Northampton County Virginia TITHABLES

1662-1677

John B. Bell

HERITAGE BOOKS
2008

HERITAGE BOOKS
AN IMPRINT OF HERITAGE BOOKS, INC.

Books, CDs, and more—Worldwide

For our listing of thousands of titles see our website at
www.HeritageBooks.com

Published 2008 by
HERITAGE BOOKS, INC.
Publishing Division
100 Railroad Ave. #104
Westminster, Maryland 21157

Copyright © 1993 John B. Bell

Other books by the author:
Northampton County, Virginia Tithables, 1720-1769

All rights reserved. No part of this book may be reproduced or transmitted in any form or by any means, electronic or mechanical, including photocopying, recording or by any information storage and retrieval system without written permission from the author, except for the inclusion of brief quotations in a review.

International Standard Book Numbers
Paperbound: 978-1-55613-893-5
Clothbound: 978-0-7884-7286-2

TABLE OF CONTENTS

YEAR	STARTING ON PAGE
FOREWORD	v
1662	1
1663	6
1664	9
1665	15
1666	21
1667	27
1668	33
1669	missing
1670	missing
1671	39
1672	missing
1673	missing
1674	45
1675	53
1676	60
1677	66

FOREWORD

The foreword to *"Northampton County, Virginia Tithables 1720-1769"* indicated an awareness only one additional, seventeenth-century tithables list (for 1666) was known and already published by *"The Virginia Historical Magazine"*. Two known lists (1667 and 1674) remained unpublished from the early Order Books. Since then, known lists, called to our attention, have included lists for 1662-1669, 1671 and 1674-1677, buried, largely unknown, in early Order Books. These include the published list for 1666 and the two unpublished lists of which we knew. The undersigned first learned of the existence of the unknown lists when they were cited as references by John R. Pagan of the University of Arkansas in his draft of the history of Homesett Plantation in Northampton County. The large volume of unpublished tithables material seemed to be enough to make transcription and publication useful to researchers.

The transcriber especially appreciates the special efforts of Mrs. E. E. Mihalyka of Cheriton, Virginia to make readable photocopies of the originals with which he could work.

The earliest lists give only the numerical number of total tithables. Later lists include heads-of-households and those (by name) tithable with them. Negroes are sometimes listed 'in toto', not by name. Sometimes the family name, less often the Christian name, is omitted for servants. The nationality, or occupation (if not a farmer) is often listed. A "drifter", perhaps passing through, is named on one list as a "sojourner". These lists are sometimes badly torn, or blotted, or faded, or difficult to read, or poorly written but, nevertheless, revealing. They are offered as near as possible to the original othography. These lists, transcribed as follows, complete the published record.

                                    John B. Bell
                                    Williamsburg, Virginia

"A List of Tithables in Northampton County Adom 1662." (Northampton County OB p. 138, f. 139, 1662.)

Coll. Edm: Scarborough

2 Coopers (in all 14 to be abated)	
4 Shoemakers	
3 Woodworkers	
1 Carpenter	
2 Salt boylers	
2 Taylors	
Other Persons	12
Dr. Geo: Clarke	7
Tho: Fowkes	5
Jno Renney	5
Wm Chase	2
Jno Drummond	2
Mr. Hugh Yeo	7
widow Bayley	5
Mr. Devorix Browne	9
Rich: Hill	7
Teage Andrews	2
Edw: Revell	4
Jno Alfons	2
Jno: Manuell	2
Tobias Selvey	1
Nath: Bradford	5
Jno Wise	6
Dorman Sellawan	2
Anto Johnson	2
Jno: Watts	2
Folcat Obin	2
Mich: Ricketts	2
Adam Taylor	1
Mr. Anto Hodgekins	4
Wm. Taylor	2
Wm. Jordan	10
Jno Parker	5
Tho: Newton	4
Majr Jno Tilney	4
Wm Smith	3
Tho: Browne	8
Jno Robinson	1
Tho: Wally	1
Jno Prettyman	
Jeffery Marshall	4
Samll James	
Jno Smith	2
Tho: Carnell	2
Edm: Kelly	2
Robt. Hirkinson	1
Henry White	1
Robt. Hill	2
Jno Evans	2
Mr. Denwood	3
Jno Paramore	4
Rich: Cox	1
Phillip Fisher	3
Wm Bosman	3

Jnº Walthom	7		Timothy Coe	4
Capt. Geo: Parker	7		Henry Scott	1
Jhº Bronx	2		Elias Hawkines	5
Jno: Williams	4		Mr. Dolby	
Geo: Truett	3		Olester Southland	4
Christopher Calvert	3		Rich: Jacob	10
Thomas Tunnell	1		Daniell Quillion	3
Jnº Ricketts	2		Jnº Johnson	1
Rich: Bundick	3		Lambert Groton	1
Robt. Richard Sen.	3		Jnº Haggaman	1
Jnº: Pratt	1		Jnº Peper	1
James Atkinson	3		Jnº King	2
Robt. Huett	5		Wm Roberts	4
Robt. Bayley	2		Daniell Etion	2
Jnº: Shipway	2		Mr. Westerhouse	3
Alphanso Ball	2		Geo: Bower	1
Henry Voss	7		Mr. Foxcroft	3
Jnº Lewis	6		Wm Gaskins	2
Robt. Kellum	6		David Wheatly	2
Jnº Whitehead	1		Sampson Robins	2
Tho: Bullock	1		Adolph Johnson	1
Geo: Smith	1		Peter Long	2
Rich: Nelson	1		James Davis	4
Robt. Watson	1		Jnº Vines	5
Henry Fields	4		Martin Otupp	1
Giles Crape	1		Tho: Smith	1

Jnº Winberry	3	Abram Vansalt	1
Jnº Furns	2	Jnº Mapp	3
Nath: Cownson	4	Rich: Granger	3
Wm Rodolphus		Mr. Wm Spencer	10
Jnº Paramore	3	Tho: Selby	1
Geo: Johnson	5	Mr. Tho: Riding	5
Alexander Addison	3	Wm Marshall	2
James Price	2	Mr. Wm Jones	4
Jno: Cobb	2	Jnº Plumb	1
Jnº Fawsett	3	Hugh Baker	1
Rich: Stephens	1	Jnº Johnson	1
Jnº Ratlife	3	Phillip Mongon	1
Tho: Bloyce	3	Capt. Jnº Savage	6
Tho: Marshall	2	Jnº Rynene	2
Jnº Waller	5	Roger Spring	1
Jnº Thompson	4	Antº Raboone	2
Arthur Upshott	5	Tho: Church	1
Benjª Lawrence	3	Jnº Basy	1
Henry Bishop	6	Wm Hudson	1
Edwd Smith	1	Robt. Downes	1
Henry Edwards	5	Robt. Cattline	2
Henry Armitrading	4	Dunkin Magnabb	1
Rich: Patrick	3	Jnº Pash	1
Wm Bashell	4	Rich: Ast	1
Tho: Alligood	1	James Bruce	2
James Sanders	2	Thomas Dimer	6
Mathew Pele	3	Antº Dolmius	2

Wm Palmer	1		Wm Lawrance	2
James Pettijohn	2		Tho: Dupark	1
Rich: Nottingham	2		Mr. Wm Kendall	10
Geo: Meridith	1		Francis Pettit	2
Edw: Gunter	2		George Freshwater	3
Rich: Clark	2		Mannuell Driggs	2
Simon Foskue	2		Mathew Pippen	1
Armestrong Foster	2		Alex Mill	1
Wm Burton	1		Capt. Edw: Littleton	12
Walter Mills	2		and at Nantua	5
Jnº Stockly	3		Jeremy Griffeth	3
Wm Stevens	2		Jnº Roberts	3
James Barnaby	3		Wm Starling	1
Edw: Smith	3		Wm Gelding	1
Edw: Stevens	2		Mr. Jnº Michael	12
Walter Price	2		Teague Odeare	3
Wm Harper	1		Robt. Warren	2
Gilbert Skinner	1		John Waterson	6
Thomas Scott	1		Neale Mackmillion	1
Nick: Powell	2		Robt. Haies	
Mr. Nelson	4		Wm Ennis	1
Robt. Johnson Sen	2		Tho: Poynter	1
Jnº Wilkins			Mark Manloe	2
Major Wm Watson			Jnº Gosall	1
Jnº Stevens			Tho: Blacklock	1
Tho: Leatherberry			Nath: Wilkins	3
Capt. Wm Andrews			Rich: Hanby	1
Mr. Jnº Custis			Jnº Daniell	4

Cristop: Turner	Paull Trendall	2
Jnᵒ Allen	Usbich Sanders	2
Teage Obohell	James Walker	3
Tho: Harmonson	Jnᵒ Frizell	1
Jnᵒ Webb	Jeremy Robinson	3
	Francis Harper	1
	Jnᵒ Severne	5
	Mathew Gething	2
	Cristop: Dixon	2
	Geo: Frizell	1
	Jnᵒ Gray	1
	Tho: Clay	2
	Wm Smith	1
	Ambrose London	4
	Thomas Bunton	2
	Robert Woods	1
	George Smith	2
	Jnᵒ Bagwell	2
	Robt. Marriott	3
	Thomas Moore	3

"A List of Tithaables in Northampton County Adom: 1663." (OB VIII, pp. f 175, p. 176, 1663.)

Mr. Jnº Dolby	2	Henry Field	1
Sampson Robins	1	Mr. Isaac Foxcroft	12
Adolph Johnson	1	Tho: Bullock	2
Jnº Whitehead	1	Wm Stevens	1
Arthur Upshott	7	Peter Covington	4
Henry Armtrading	8	James Davis	6
Mr. Wm Spencer	13	James Sanders	2
Gilbert Henderson	2	Edw: Gunter	2
Francis Darling	1	Rich: Clark	2
Daniel Wheatly	4	Thomas Estmee	1
Rich: Nottingham	2	Jnº Storkly	2
Wm Gascoine	4	Benjamen Cowdery	1
Rich: Allen	4	Armstone Foster	2
Wm Palmer	1	Cornelius Berry	1
John ?	2	Aron Francee Jacob Jacobson	2
Geo: Meridith	1		
Mr. Wm Jones	4	Jnº List	1
Rich: Granger	3	Mr. Wm Melling	5
Rich: Patrick	3	Nich: Powell	3
Abram Vansault	1	Mr. Jnº Michael	11
Coll. Jnº Stringer	7	Ushiah Sanders	4
Mr. Tho: Ryding	4	Jnº Waterson	3
Tho: Dimer	3	Robt. Marriott	3
Capt. Savage	7	Jerom Griffeth	2
James Bruce	2	Paull Trendall	3
Dunkin Magnab	1	Emanuell Druggs	3
Tho: Harmonson	6	Wm Starling	1

Edw: Smith	4	Rich: Merrychip	1
Rich: Ast	1	Robt. Dumell	1
Wm Lawrance	2	Robt. Hutchinson	3
Rich: Depark	1	Lt. Coll. Wm Waters	10
Roger Spring	1	Teage Odeare	3
Jn° Abbott	2	Tho: Blacklock	2
Wm Webster	1	Robt. Warren	2
Tho: Church	2	Major Wm Andrews	2
Sam¹¹ Young	2	Prince Wilson	3
Robt. Catlin	1	Wm South	1
Wm Hudson	2	Rich: Whitmarsh	4
Wm Boyst	2	Jeremy Robins	5
Ani: Lamus	1	Mark Manlon	2
ChristPer: Turnor	2	Edague Binghell	2
ChristPer: Stanly	4	Wm Janis	3
Daniell Jackson	1	Jn° Allen	2
Jn° Patch	1	Mr. Wm Custis	4
Jn° Plumb	2	Thomas Hunt	4
Edw: Stevens	3	Bashaw (Negro & wife)	2
John Webb	8	John Stevens & Wm Cason	2
Andrew Small	4	Thomas Swindall	1
Neale Mackmilling	3	Jn° Forsith (& a woman Slave)	2
Francis Payne	2	Mathew Gething	3
Mr. John Roberts	6	Francis Harper	2
Jn° Daniell	4	Jn° Gray	1
Edw: Dolby	3	Jn° Browne	4
Emanuell Hall	1	Jn° Knight	1

Rich: Hanby	1	Gilbert Skiner	1
Jno: Marshall	1	Wm Harper	3
James Bonwell	5	Tho: Moore	5
Nath: Wilkins	4	Alexander Mill	1
Robt. Blake	3	George Smith	1
Jnº Wilkins	1	George Frizell	1
Mrs. Grace Robins	11	Christ: Per: Dixon	3
Lt. Coll Wm. Kendall	10	Tho: Scott	1
George Esdall	1	George Freshwater	3
Wm & Luke Gelding	2	Thomas Harmer	8
Henry Hopgins	1	Mathew Pippin	2
Edw: Parker	2	Jnº Gosall	1
Tho: Clay	1	Ambross London	9
Tho: Dunton	3	James Walker	2
Mr. Jnº Custis	18	King Tony	2

"A List of Tithables in Northampton County - An° Dom 1664." (OB VIII, f. 197, p. 198, f. 198, 1664).

Mr. Isaac Foxcroft	9!	Martin Oates	1
Henry Hall			
Rich: Ridge		Jn° Stockley	4
Patrick (Irish)		Abraham Heeth	
Phillip (Irish)		Jn° Bowin	
Jack (Indian)		Tho: Estmeath	
Humphrey Grinshane			
Sisley (Negroes!)		Richard Clark	2
		Tegue Harman	
Gilbert Henderson	2		
Edward Joyne		Adoleif Johnson	1
Arthur Upshott	6	Rich: Nottingham	2
Tho: Jacob		Wm Ewin	
Tho: Gething			
Henry Reade		William Palmer	1
Rich: Jeffers			
Wm Abdin		Mr. Cowdrey	5
		Tho: Kendall	
James Davis	5	Josias Cowdrey	
Peirce Davis		Bryan Caherne	
Tho: Davis		Mathew Pate	
Jn° Dolby			
Abraham Bonn			
		Armstrong Foster	2
James Sanders	2	Joseph Godwin	
James Glaswell			
		Jn° Clarke	1
Capt. Wm Jones	4		
Charles Holden		Paull Winbrow	1
John ____			
Mary Mass			
		Rich: Allen	2
Nicholas Hudson	2	Jn° Sterling	
John Winbrow			
		Geo: Smith	1
Sampson Robins	4		
Amos Garris		Jn° Evans	1
Isaac Russell			
Lambert Grouten		Henry Field	4
		Jn° Field	
Peter Lang	3	Robt. Miller	
Steven Lang		Jeremy Walker	
Cornelius Berry			
		Tho: Bullock	1
Thomas Dunton	2		
white maid		Geo: Boxer	1
Rich: Dibbins	1	Wm Westerhouse	5
		Henrick Hagaman	
William Stevens	2	Jn° Denny	
Richard Richards		Lambner Githins	
		Enert Johnson	

John Vines	4		
Robt. Foster		Wm Satchell	2
Wm Foster		Daniell Paine	
Phillip Jacob			
		John Coale	2
Edw: Gunter	1	Peter Viker	
Francis Darling	1	James Pettyjohn	2
		Robert Twilly	
Simon Foskue	2		
Tho: Foskue		Thomas Dimmer	4
		Durman Mahowin	
Wm Gaskins	6	Jonathan Nutt	
Robt. Gaskins		Anthony Blar	
Jnº Foster			
Wm Rubbish		George West	3
Robt. Butler		Tho: Cottingham	
Negro woman		Daniell Woodgate	
Walter Mills	2	Richard Ast	2
Tho: Howard		Miles Graves	
Browne Henricks	1	Samuell Younge	2
		John Abbott	
John Dolby	8		
Denis Oder		John Mapp	2
Jnº Andrews		Tho: Colling	
Jnº Scammell			
Tho: Johnson		Edward Stevens	4
Hen: Marshall		Wm Hickman	
Devorˣ Costin		Jnº Wilson	
Tho: Brookes		Joseph Hickman	
Capt. Wm Spencer	15	Nich: Granger	2
Patrick Stmelly		Jnº Robins	
Tho: Bagley			
Robert Wiggin		Edw: Smith (Constable)	2
Tho: Powell		Edw: Vaughan	
Jnº Simens		William Louim	
Cornelius Harman			
Wm Scriven		Mrs. Ryding	3
5 Negroes		Argoll Yardly	
Nich: Sallaman		Wm Vaughan	
David Mahane		Katanna (Negro)	
Ellias Hartry	7	Richard Patrick	2
George Subith		Tho: Ast	
Jnº Furnier			
Tege Oregon		Richard Dupark	1
B Queen			
Jacob Hill		Phillip Mongon	1
Henry Newton			
		Wm Lannenore	2
		Tho: Berrisford	

Coll. Jnº Stringer	7			
Jnº Tatum				
Tho: Payne		Jnº Plumb		2
Theophilus Boulton		Abram Shepheard		
Jnº Hornsby				
Tho: Oxford		Thomas Harmanson		7
Jno: Bulle		Edw: Cable		
		Danˡˡ Cawle		
Robt. Harrison	1	George Jenkins		
		Wm Sharpe		
Wm Hudson	2	James Greenewood		
Benjamine Canutus		Jnº Morranis		
Jnº Patch	1	William Webster		2
		Samuell Webster		
Tho: Duparke	2			
Danˡˡ Donnehough		ChristPer: Stanly		2
		Wm Jones		
Tho: Church	1			
		Walter Price		2
Richard Jester	1	Wm Kennitt		
Lt. Coll. Wm Kendall	8	Jnº Savage		3
Danˡˡ Bakeer		Edw: Olfely		
Jnº Kendall		Daniell Cleary		
Jnº Abraham				
Mathew Williams		Mrs Robins (her family)		9
Wm. Harmon		Andrew Small		
Charles (Negro)		Walter Mathews		
Mingo (Negro)		Wm Lyme		
		Wm Padgett		
Jnº Webb	4	Jnº Simons		
Jnº Margretts		Jnº Wootyens		
Jnº Williams		Anthony (Negro)		
Henry Lurton		Jack (Negro)		
		Jone (Negro)		
Robt. Burrell	2			
Bartholemew Cosier		Jnº Marshall		1
Neal Mackmillion	2	Jan Malytheis		1
John Jennett				
		Mr. Jnº Robins		5
John Daniell	5	John (Negro)		
Thomas Owin		Congo (Negro)		
Jack (Negro)		Cosongo (Negro)		
Aron (Negro)		Elizabeth (Negro)		
Shilla Dennis				
		George Mortimer		1
Robert Blake	2			
John Jackson				

		Lt. Coll. Wm Waters	8
		Richard Lewit	
Charles Perkes	2	Richard Tull	
Jnº Walter		Henry Mills	
		Morgan Jones	
Thomas Shepheard	1	Edward Jones	
		Lawrence Henry	
Richard Hamby	1	Bess (a Negro)	
Jnº Wilkins	1	Thomas Peck	1
Emanuell Hall	2	John Badum	1
Cornelius Areall			
		Eustis Sanders	2
Francis Payne	1	Jonathan Gilly	
Jnº Francisco	2	Wm Starling	2
Cristian Francisco		Henry Morgam	
Francis Pettitt	2	John Leift	1
Tho: Heady			
		Robert Marriott	2
Jacob Bishopp	3	Richard Tatlock	
Jnº Dormon			
Wm Savage		Teage Odeare	1
Nathaniell Wilkins	3	Pearce Delling	2
Jnº Wilshire		Dennis Omalegon	
Geo. (Negro)			
		Wm Gelding (Constable)	1
Mrs. Voss	1	Luke Gelding	
a Negro woman			
		Manuell Rodriggs	1
Robert Warren	2	Tho: Blacklock	1
Joseph Warren			
		John Waterson	4
Mr. Jnº Michael	16	Jnº Floyd	
Jnº Michael		Antº Taylor	
Harman (a cooper)		Jacob Glanfield	
Rowland (a Servt)			
Wm Gray		Howell Glading	1
Jnº Allworth			
Peter Fonteyn		Jerom Griffeth	2
William (Negro)		Wm Cord	
Anthony (Negro)			
John (Negro)		Paull Trendalll	2
Mingo (Negro)		Steven Anis	
Ellis (Negro)			
Bando (Negro)		Cristopher Dixon	3
Frank (Negro)		Benomy Ward	
Dennis (Negro)		Tho: Emanuell	
Nanny (Negro)			

My Sloops men Omitted and   -
Thomas Goodame whome I
conceive not to be listed heere.
Pronis Nelson   2
  James Carter

Major Wm Andrews   2
  Thomas Farnell

Mr. Wm Melling   6
  Robt. Githins
  Henry Hopgood
  Jnº Mackintosh
  Arthur Bowser
  Mark Venam

Nicholas Powell   3
  Edw: Handcock
  Derman Naliqulin

Capt. Jnº Custis   18
  Jnº Martin
  Benjamine Perry
  Wm Barton
  Cornelius Morris
  George Lilly
  Tho: Shoemaker
  Charles Winefred
  Jnº Taylor
  Wm Senior
  Daniell (Negro)
  Gabriell (Negro)
  Bob (Negro)
  Bess (Negro)
  Wm Clemmons
  Mall (Negro)
  Joane (Negro)
  Daniell Swindall

Gilbert Skiner   2
  and Wm Thomas

Wm Harper   2
  Richard Quinch

Alexander Mills   1

George Frizell   1

Robert Hayes   2
  Joseph Cooke

Bastian Cane   2
  King Toney

Bastian Fernando   2
  Thomas Swindall

John Stevens   1

Jnº Foxsith   2
  Abraham Collins

Mathew Pipin   1

Thomas Clay   1

John Severne   4
  Peter Severne
  John Farthing
  Rich: Barnet

John Gething   2
  Howell

Francis Harper   2
  Walter Caerter

George Freshwater   2
  Dy (a Negro)

Thomas Scott   2
  Jnº Owen

Mrs. Littletons family   5
  Paull Carter
  and wife
  John Warper
  Peter George (Negro)
  ould Jack (Negro)

George Smith   2
  Jnº Cropley

Jnº Bagwell   3
  Tho: Bagwell
  Christ: Per: Nutter

Rich: Whitmarsh   4
  Francis Roberts
  Robt. Hollyday
  Samuell Janett

Thomas Poynter   10
  Jnº Gray
  Wm Lewis
  Jnº Watts
  Fran: Savidge
  Griffeth Win
  Tho: Driggos
  James (Negro)
  Manja (Negro)
  Katrina (Negro)

Jnº Fenebee   1

Anbross London   4
  Ellis Appme
  Wm Connelay
  Tho: Coleman

Mr. Wm Custis   3
  Wm Baker
  Wm Jerman

Edward Sacker   1

George Esdall   1

Mark Mmanlove   3
  Eustis Persons
  Tho; Manlove

Jeremy Robins   4
  Wm Briggs
  Wm Soar
  Judith (Negro)

Thomas Hunt   4
  Thomas Gilly
  Jnº Jullop
  Jnº Daniell

Teague Obohell   2
  Derman Joy

Thomas Moore   7
  Thomas Hogg
  Jnº Moore
  Wm Allum
  Tho: Sumerfeild
  James Burkett
  Bess (minor)

Wm Ennis   2
  Ed: Ennis

Tho: Harmon   1

Jnº Knight   2
  Donman Olanman

Mr. Teakles family
  Tho: Teackle   3 sic
  Tho: Hall
  Dermon Laughling
  Jnº Teague
  Richard Mibble
  Ed: Brakhouse
  Jnº Luke
  George Russell
  Robt. Shepheard
  Ann Harmon
  Whereof 6 Persons
  & and himself to be deducted
  by Act of Assembly

"... of tithables in North:ton County Anno Domi 1665 Delivered in a Court held in the sd County the 4th of September 1665." (Book X, p. 14-15, 1664-74.)

Mr Edward Gunter	3	Adolph Johnson	2
Thomas Ast		Thomas Wright	
Richard Wildgoose			
		Mr. John Dolby	7
Teague Harman	1	John Andrews	
		Thomas Wilson	
Richard Dibbins	1	Cornelius Arealle	
		Thomas Johnson	
Walter Mills		John Scallamore	
		Derick Coffin	
Richard Nottingham	2		
William Ewins		Mr. William Westerhaye	5
		Henrick Waggaman	
Beniamine Cowdree	3	Lawrence Sillyer	
Lambert Groton		William Holstead	
Josias Cowdree		Adrian Westerhouse	
Armstrong Foster	3	Peter Watson	2
Joseph Goddin		Matthew Holt att John	
Thomas Evens		Furrs (the Constable)	
Samson Robin	3	Richard Allen	3
Thomas Bagley		John Starlinge	
Robert Moore		John Denny	
James Sanders	3	William Satchell	1
Bryan Terherne			
John Glaswell		John Field	5
		Jeremia Walter	
James Davis	7	George Sutch	
Thomas Davis		Isaack Russell	
Pierce Davis		Stephen Avis	
James Davis			
Abraham Winsey		Mr. Arthur Upshott	7
Robert Higgins		Phillipp Jacob	
Stephen Lange		Leonard House	
		Henry Reade	
Mr. ?	7	Thomas Jacoh	
John ?		Rich: Rakes	
Teague ?		Tho: Gethings	
?			
John ?amberling		Mr. Isaack Foxcraft	12
Henry Newton		Danill Foxcraft	
Owen Morgan		Roberts	
		Richard Ridge	
Mr. Arthur Armitradinge	5	Patrick (Irish)	
Morgan Polding		Phillipp (Irish)	
James Brookes		Patrick (Irish)	
John Davison		Jack (Indian)	
Will: Wood		3 Negroes	
		Donnack Damins	

Thomas Do?	2		
Robert Will?		Mr. Thomas Rideinge	6
		John Lyon	
Henry Hill	2	Henry Mathews	
Edw: Joyne		Thomas Trowfiss	
		William Vaughan	
Capt. William Spencer	13	Catalina (negro)	
John Synnery			
Robert Wiggan		Capt. John Savage	5
Will: Scriven		Daniell Plancy	
Nicholas Salmon		Robert F?	
Timothy Strange		John Enmis	
Patrick Shelley		Tempus Betha	
Thomas Powell			
Cornelius Harmon		Richard Patrick	4
David Mahoone		Daniell ?ina	
3 Negroes		Abraham Heath	
		John Dendy	
George Smith	1		
		William Marshall	2
Francis Darling	1	William Tipshott	
William Felix	5	William Lawrence	2
John Foster		Thomas Bedford	
Robert Foster			
John Samis		William Webster	1
William Smith			
		Jacob Bishop	1
Mr. William Gaskins	6		
Robert Gaskins		John Johnson	1
John Foster			
2 Negroes		John Plumb	1
Robert Butler			
Nath: Stockey		Robert Harrison	1
John Evens		Samuel Young	1
Richard Gilberts	2	Thomas Duparke	1
Peter Vickor			
		John Patch	1
John Coke	2		
Robert ?willy		John Abbott	1
Simon Figues	3	Abraham VanSoulte	1
Thomas Figues			
Derick Derickson		Thomas Collins	1
Mr. John Stock	4	Christopher Stanley	3
Thomas Estmeed		William Jones	
William Rabishaw		William Kermitt	
John Kevin			
		William Hickman	2
Martin Oaks	1	Joseph Hickman	

Cornelius Berry	2	Phillipp Mongon (Negro)	2
Peter Lange		his wife	
William Stevens	1	Richard Foster	1
John Whitehead	1	Francis Pettit	2
John Clark	1	John Marge?k	
John Winberow Sen	1	Edward Smith	3
		Edward Vaughan	
John Winberow Jun	1	William Owen	
Capt Willliam Joanes	3	Walter Price	2
Harman Johnson		Joseph Cooke	
John Lucas		Richard Robbins	2
Coll: John Stringer	7	Ed: Ashly	
Mr. Baugh		Edward Stephens	3
John Tatum		John a boy	
Robert ?ilne		Mathew Herne	
John Hornesly			
Thomas Oxford		William Hudson	2
Richard Curtiss		Canutus Bruse	
Thomas Church	2	Richard Ast	2
Samuell Church		Miles Graves	
Thomas Zimmer	3	Christopher Turner	2
Jonathan Newte		Nicholas Frost	
Anthony Blaz			
		John Daniell	2
Stephen Harlor	1	John (a Negro)	
Richard Duparks	1	Richard Hanby	1
Nicholas Granger	1	John Wilkins	1
Thomas Betts	1	Thomas Sheppard	1
Thomas Harminson	8	Robert Blake	2
Edward Cable		John Jackson	
Daniell Cole			
John Marrine		John Francisco (Negro)	
Geo: Jenkins		Arian his wife (Negro)	
Will: Sharpe			
Jamers Greenewood		Emanuell Hall	2
A Negro woman		John Mockentosh	
John Webb	6	Francis Pane (Negro)	1
William Morris			
John Abills		Mr. Vosse Family	4
Henry Lurton		John Floyd	
Jane Gazall		Thomas Coffin	
Ann (Negro)		Nan (a Negro)	

Nathaniel Wilkins 4
  John Wilkins
  Richard Cox
  George (a Negro)

Mr. John Robins 6
  Cornelius Morris
  Congo (Negro)
  Cogongo his wife
  John King (Negro)
  Elizab: Carter (Negro)

Charles Isaackes 5
  Joseph Isaackes
  John Walter
  Will: Smart
  Tho: Clayton

John Dorman 2
  John Ast

Leif^t. Coll. Will: Kendall 15
  Daniell Baker
  Geo: Mortimer
  John Kendall
  Will: Cord
  John Abraham
  John Harry
  Henry Barney
  Walter Manington
  Richard Richards
  Mary Knight his wife
    on PettiJohn's account
  Will: Harmor (Negro)
  Charles (Negro) a boy
  Mingo (Negro) a woman
  Aron Franses (Seaman)
  Mathew William (Seaman)

Perse Dillion 2
  Dennis Omalegon

Robert Marriott 2
  Thomas Such

Thomas Blacklock 2
  Kate (a Negro woman)

Emanuell Rodrigues (Negro) 1

Jeremia Griffith 1

Mrs. Grace Robins her family
  Andrew Small 9
  Walter Mathews
  William Savage
  William Line
  John Wootters
  William Padgett
  John Simmonds
  Anthony (a Negro)
  John Archer

Thomas Hemins 1
  (att Will: Smith's)

Will: Geldinge 2
  Luke Geldinge

Nicholas Powell 4
  Rich: Tatlock
  Derman Laughling
  Richard Williams

Will: Blare 1
  att Eustis Sanders the Constable

John Waterson 4
  Jacob Glanfield
  James Collins
  John Moore

Will: Paule 1
  att George Trendalls

Robert Warren 2
  Joseph Warren

William Starlinge 2
  Henry Morgan

Leift. Coll. Will: Waters 13
  Thomas Hedde
  Jacob Barber
  Morgan Joanes
  ? Joanes
  Jacob Chiltnam
  George Terherne
  James Stampe
  Edward Evins
  Bess (a Negro woman)
  Peter Bastianson
  Lawrence Jacobson
  Christian Kersanbrooke

Mr. John Mitchell   12
  Edw: Corkin
  Rowland Williams
  William Gray
  John Allworth
  Peter Fountaine   Richard Witmarsh   4
  Anthony (Negro)   Robert Holiday
  Bando (Negro)   Samuell Emett
  Besse (Negro)   Thomas Davis
  Nanny (Negro)
  Denis (Negro)   James Walker   2
  Areon Goggon (a German)   Christopher Stopling

William Mellinge   5 Thomas Hunt   4
  Robert Filkins   John Sallecome
  Daniell Neech   John Dannell
  Arthur Bowzer   Willliam Shower
  Joseph Senam
                                     George Isdell   1
Maior Will: Andrewes   3
  Thomas Fornell   Henry Williams   2
  Jacob Bond   John Matythies

Provice Nelson   2 Darmon Lockland   1
  Bartholemew Cosax
                                     Mr. Will: Custis   3
Capt. John Custis   16   Will: Baker
  John Robinson   John Mellony
  Mikell Stone
  Henry Forsman   Will: Ennis
  Thomas Joanes   Edward Ennis
  Charles Wrissell
  Beniamine Prezy   John Allen   2
  William Senior   Edmund Allen
  Charles Holding
  John Aldolphus   Teage Odeere   1
  Daniell (the sheppard)
  Daniel (Negro)   Mathew Pippin   1
  Gabriell (Negro)
  Bess: (Negro)   Robert Hayes   1
  Moll (Negro)
  Babb: (Negro)   Jonas Dixon   2
                                       Benony Ward
Jeremie Robinson   4
  Richard Goose   Francis Harper   2
  Robert Smith   Walter Carter
  Judith (Negro)
                                     George Frizell   1

Mr. Francis Pigott	4		
Peter (Negro)		Neale Mackmillion	2
Jack (Negro)		John Juett	
Tom (Negro)			
		Thomas Moore	5
John Bagwell	2	Tho: Hogg	
Thomas Bagwell		Tho: Summersett	
		John Moore	
Alexander Mill	1	James Buckitt	
Old King (Negro)	3	Thomas Scott	1
Busse (Negro)			
Busse's wife (Negro)		Gilbert Skinner	1
Mr. Thomas Harman	1	George Willis	1
John Stevens	1	Stephen Costen	1
Francis Robins	1	William Harper	2
		Richard Quinch	
Howell James (att Math:Gethinge)	2		
John Fatherly (Constable)		Ambrose London	6
		George Lilley	
John Owen	1	John Waple	
		George Hasford	
John Knight	2	Will: (an Irishman)	
Thomas Manuell		Ellis Upshur	
Henry Marchman	2	Mr. Thomas Teagle (Minister presenk)	
James Weatherly		Edward Douglas	3
		Thomas Hedges	
Thomas Poynter	9	Edw: Brockhouse	
John Watts		John Teage	
Denam Foy		Rich: Niblet	
William Lewis		Hinnery Picke	
John Hawkins		Joseph Aims	
Francis Savage		John Luke	
Thomas Duggins		Ann Harmon	
James (Negro)		besides himselfe 9	
Mary (Negro)		deductions 6 & himself	
		according to Act	
George Smith	2		
Dennam Plandum		Basshawe (Negro) & his wife	2
George Freshwater	2		
Dye (Negro)			

Year 1666. Original is often unreadable. See *The Virginia Historical Magazine*, Vol. 10, pp. 194-196, 258-293. (Northampton County OB f. 28, p. 29. f. 29, 1666.

Thomas Dunton	6	Edward Stevens	2
Isaack Russell		John Wilson	
Robt: Dunworth			
Wm Smith		John Lyon	2
John Pike		Tho: Collins	
Daniell Jill			
		John Mapp	2
Jeasse Harman	2	Peter Watson	
Thomas Owen			
		Wm Marshall	2
Beniamine Cowdree		Will: Tipshott	
Josias Cowdree			
Cornelius Harman		Wm Hickman	3
		Joseph Hickman	
John Kendall	7	Thomas Rice	
Owin Edmond			
George South		Mr. Tho: Ridinge	8
John Farrier		Mr. Argoll Yardly	
John Tomblings		Sam: England	
Henry Neuton		Will: Vaughanghom	
Owen Hall		Hen: Mathew	
		Griffin Morgan	
Arthur Armitradinge		Tho: Rock	
Isaack Jacob		Catalina (a Negro)	
Thomas Needy			
John Dawson		Abraham Vansoult	1
Francis Broukes			
Steven Avis		Nicholas Granger	3
Morgan Pouldin		Thomas Wilson	
Wm Stevens		John Robins	
Henry Reade			
Derick Derickson		Cannlus Pence	1
		John Abbott	1
Peter Lang	2		
Cornelius George		Phillipp Mongon (Negro)	2
		Mary Mongon his wife (Negro)	
John Dolby Sr.	5		
John Dolby Jr.		George West	1
John Scamell			
Hen: Bowans		Richd Ast	3
Rich: Costinge		Miles Growk	
		Robt: Warbeton	
John Cole	4		
John Field		Jacob Bishopp	2
Robt: Twilly		Rich: Bibbins	
Wm Rabisshaw			
		John Plumb	1

Thomas Bagley	1		
James Sanders	3	Tho: Church	2
Perse Davis		Sam: Church	
John Dolby			
		Thomas Parker	2
		John Hornby	
Henry Hall	1		
		Duncan Macknabb	1
Leift. Isaack Foxcroft	8		
Phillipp (Irishman)		John Basy	1
Patrick (Irishman)			
Thomas Lucas		Robt: Harrison	2
4 Negroes		Robt: Hopkins	
Rich: Nottingham	2	Abraham Sheppard	1
Wm Ewin			
		Edward Cable	1
Thomas Ast	1		
		Will: Lawrence	2
att the widdow Gunters	2	Tho: Berisford	
Rich: Wildegoose			
Tony (a Frenchman)		Rich: Dupark (att Wibly's)	1
Simon Focus Sen.	4	Will: Kennitt	1
Simon Focus Jun.			
Thomas Focus		Thomas Dimmer	2
Mathew Patrick		Tho: Nabe	
Walter Mills	1	Rich: Patrick	2
		John Denby	
John Winbrough Sen.	3		
John Winbrough Jun.		Richard Jester	1
Frank Winbrough			
		Coll: John Stringer	6
Cap: Wm Spencer	9	John Tatum	
Wm. Whittington		Robt: Chew	
Robt Wiggin		David Gaime	
Wm Scriven		Rich: Curtesse	
Jacob Hill		Tho: Oxford	
Patrick Strelby			
Thomas Powell		Joseph Godwin	2
Two Negroes		Ceasar Godwin	
Mr. Wm Westerhouse	1	Abraham Heath	1
Lawrence Schyn	4	Capt: John Savage	6
Adryan Westerhouse		John Amis	
John Richards		Edw: Ashby	
Armstrong Foster		Robt: Tygar	
		Tempus Betha	
Mr. Thomas Evens	2	Signy Feild	
Mr. Haggaman			

Francis Pettitt	2		
Justiman Pettitt		Will: Paule	1
Christopher Stanley	1	Tho: Blacklock	1
Joseph Parkes	4	Dennis Omalegon	1
Wm Gilsby			
Wm Smart		Wm Mellinge	6
Tho: Claydon		Robt: Jilkin	
		Arthur Bowzer	
Nath: Wilkins	3	Peter Vickar	
Rich: Cox		Isaack Venam	
George (Negro man)		John Wyer	
John Daniel	4	Joseph Warren	1
James Bowzer			
Wm Edmunds		Jerom Griffith	1
Black Jack (Negro)			
		Tho: Sheppard	1
Rich: Hanby	1		
		Province Nelson	2
Thomas Harminson	7	Daniel Paine	
Daniel Call			
John Manninge		Richard Whitmarsh	5
Wm Jenkins		Wm Wathum	
Wm Sharpe		Robt: Holliday	
John Wills (att mill)		Sam: Ames	
Nan (Negro woman)		Tho: Davis	
John Dorman	2	Harman Johnson	2
Roger Kirkman		John Mathis	
att Mrs. Robins	6	James Walker	3
John Margetts		Hen: Williams	
Rich: Robins Jun.		Rich: Tatlock	
John Symonds			
John Wooters		Mr. Tho: Hunt	4
John Archer (Negro)		John Follicome	
Tony (Negro)		John Darnell	
		Wm Shore	
Robt: Blaks	2		
John Jackson		John Bagwell	1

Mr. John Robins
  Tho: Parnell
  John Kinge (Negro)
  3 Negroes
	6	Thomas Bagwell	1

		Capt. John Custis
		  John Robinson
		  Michael Stone
			15

Walter Mathews
  Andrew Smaw
  Wm Savage
	3	Tho: Joanes
		  Charles Weissell
		  Hen: Foreman
		  Daniell Swindall	

Wm Lyne
  Wm Padgett
	2	Beniamine Perry
		  George Lilly
		  John Wappell
		  5 Negroes	

Maj. Wm Andrews
  John Andrews
  John Pirce
	3	Robert Hayes	1

		Teage Odeer	1
George Isdell	1	Mathew Pippin	1

Nicholas Powell
  Dexmon Hardlins
  Richard Williams
	3	Jeremia Robinson
		  Robt: Smith
		  Judith (Negro)
			3

Will: Smith
  Tho: Hennige
	2	Mr. Francis Pigott
		  Peter (Negro)
			5

John Wilkins
  John Floyd
	2	John (Negro)
		  Thomas (Negro)
		  Jane (Negro)	

John Waterson Jacob Glassfield	4	Kinge Tony (Negro)	1
John Wiltshire John More		Bastian Cane (Negro)	1

Will: Starlinge
  Tho: Turnell
	4	Thomas Betts
		  Tho: Colman
			2

Hen. Morgan John Willett		Ellis Aphugh	1
att Mathew Gettinge's Constable Walter Carter	3	Thomas Swindall	1
Howell James John Fathery		Bassaur (Negro)	1
		Mr. Thomas Harman	1
Francis Harper	1	Stephen Coffin Benoni Ward	2
George Frizell	1		
Dormman Loffland	1	Thomas Clay	1
		John Stevens	1
Alex: Mills Rich: Core	2	Geo: Willis	1

John Adolph	4	Thomas Hogg	2
Wm Cord		Abraham Collins	
Jonas Dixon			
Derman Fox		Neale Mackmillins	2
		John Jewett	
Tho: Scott	2		
John Watts		Geor: Smith	2
		Wm Lewis	
Thomas Moore	5		
John Owen		John Allen	2
John Moore		Edm: Allen	
John Somersett			
James Bookett		att the widdow Hall's	1
		Hen: Michael	
Wm Harper	2		
Rich: Quinch		Wm Ennis	2
		Edward Ennis	
Geo: Freshwater	2		
Dic (a Negro)		Hen. Marshmant	3
		James Weatherly	
John Knight	1	Wm Baker	
Tho: Poynter	8	copied (some above, all below) from
John Hawkins		Va. Hist. Mag. because original is torn
Tho: Driggus (Negro)		and peices are missing:
Rich: Richardson			
Mary his wife		Will: Gatehill	2
Derman Olandum		John Evans	
Francis Driggus (Negro)			
James Driggus (Negro)		Nicholas Hudson	1
John Francisco (Negro)	2	John Faris	2
Arisbian His Wife (Negro)		Clause (a Dutch boy)	
Lieft. Coll Wm Kendall.	14	Edward Joyne	1
Daniel Baker			
Geo: Mortimer		Wm Gaskin	5
John Abraham		Robt: Gaskin	
John Parsons		Robt: Butler	
John Harris		Nath: Starkey	
Jeter Morgan		Nat (Negro)	
Morgan Thomas			
Geo: Massy		Thomas Bulluck	1
Walter Mannington			
Mingo (Negro)		Sampson Robins	2
Charles (Negro)		Rich: Ridge	2
Aron Franscon (Seaman)			
Mathew Williams (Seaman)		Amos Garris	1
Att Wilkcox	1	John Walter	2
Lambet Groton		Jeremiah Walter	
Christopher Turner	1	Will: Morris	1

```
Att M. Vosses                    2
   Thos: Loffing
   Nan (Negro woman)          Jas: Davis Sen.                    5
                                   Jas: Davis Jun.
Mr. John Michael            12     Thomas Davis
   Ed: Lockitt                     Steven Lang
   Peter Fountaine                 Abraham Bownamy
   John Aleworth
   Rowland Williams                Capt. Will Joanes             4
   William Gray                    John Lukes
   Anthony Joanes                  John Bulluck
   Anthony (Negro)                 Harman Johnson
   Banelo (Negro)
   Frank (Negro)                   Wm: Hamon (Negro)             2
   Dennisse (Negro)                Jane Hamon (Negro)
   Ann (Negro)
                                   Wm Geldinge                   3
Bartholemew Cosier           2     Luke Geldinge
   Francis Roberts                 Charles Geldinge

Leift. Coll. Wm Waters      10     John Webb                     5
   Peter Bastianson                John Glassell
   Lawrence Jacobson               Hen: Lartin
   Tho: Reade                      Cornelius Areale
   Edw: Joanes                     Nan (Negro woman)
   Jacob Chilton
   Geo: Terherne                   Francis Jane (Negro)          1
   Ed: Evans (Att Hopkins)
   Sam Handee                      Manuel Drigg (Negro)          1
   William (Negro)
   Bill (Negro)                    Willis Saunders               2
                                   Daniel Keeth
```

"A List of Tythables in North^ton County in Virginia delivered at a Court held in the s^d County the 4th September 1667." Original very faint - partly unreadable. (Northampton County OB f. 41, p. 42, f. 42, 1667).

Samson Robins	2		Rich: Nottingham	2
Geo: Bonum			Wm Scott	
Amos Garris	1		Wm ?	1
Henry Reade	3		Nath: ?	2
Morgan Poullen			Robt. ?	
Will: Stevens				
			John Furrs	2
John Haggaman	1		Ralph Warnell	
Mathew Patrick	3		Wm Stockely	3
Rita Watkins			John Davis	
Teage Haman			John Satchell	
Robt: Miller	1		Peter ?	2
			Tho: ?	
John Abraham	6			
Tho: Wilson			James ?	6
Nicholas Sherwood			Edward ?	
Ben: Jeffery			John (a serv^t)	
Wm Beder			John Robins	
Arthur Upshott			Abraham Smaw	
			James ?	
Robt: Blades	2			
Isaac Jacob			John Feild	5
			Mathew Hayes	
John Dason	4		John D?	
Francis Brookes			a Servant Boy	
Stephen Avis			John Andrews	
Arthur Armitrading				
			Paule Wimborough	2
Phillip Jacob	2		John Wimborough Sen	
Tho: Bullock				
			John Wimborough Jun	1
John Dolby	2			
James Sandes			S? Foscue	3
			Jacob Gill	
John Senus	1		Simon Foscue	
Tho: Bagley	1		Steven Howell	5
			John Thornell	
			Isaack Russell	
Brian Keherne	2		Feny Newton	
John Wanier			John Kendall	
John Dolby Jun	5		Thomas Evans	2
John Skamell			Armstrong Foster	
John Beck				
Derick Johnson			Richard Gilbert	1
John Dolby Junr				

Stephen Lang	2		John Evans	1
Peter Lang				
			John Whitehead	1
Robt: Gaskins	5			
Robt: Butler			Armstrong Foster	3
Nath: Stalkey			John Smith	
a Negro woman			Wm Foster	
Wm Gaskins				
			Tho: ?	2
Adrian Westerhuose	5		Hen: Hill	
Lawrence ?				
Wm Westerhouse			Jeremy Walter	1
John Garris				
Wm Westerhouse			Patrick Stally	3
			Rich: Wildegoose	
Josias Cowdree	4		Robt: Wildegoose	
Wm Cowdree				
? Harman			Tho: Agil	1
Ben: Cowdree				
			Francis Roberts	1
Tho: Estmeed	1			
			Geo: Bo?r	1
Francis Darling	1			
			Hen: Forse	8
Thomas Norley	1		Peter Fountinell	
			David Price	
John ?	1		John Hars?	
			Tony (Negro)	
? Johnson	4		Humphry (Negro)	
? Loyd			Susan (Negro)	
Tho: Lang			Lieft. Isaac Foxcroft	
Capt Wm Jones				
			Richard Dibbins	1
Walter Mills	1			
			Sam: Young	1
George South	10			
Wm S?			Walter Price	1
Wm P?				
Henry			Robert Harrison	3
? ?			Robt. Hopkins	
John Collins			John Parsons	
? (a Negro)				
Tho: ?			Tho: Duparkes	1
Capt. Wm Spencer				
			Rich: Duparkes	2
? Dimner	4		Peter Duparkes	
? Newton				
Robert Groton			Capt. John Savage	6
Wm ?			Rich: Robins	
			Sydny Field	
? ?	1		Tho: Banks	
			John Ames	
Christopher Stanley	1		Tempus Bethy	

Nicholas Granger John Lucas	2	Richard Foster Sam: Powell	2
Rich: Patrick John Darby	2	Edward Cable	1
Abraham Heath	1	Joseph Godwin Ceasar Godwin	2
Edward Steven Wm Jipshott? John ?	3	Mr. Thomas Ridinge Mr. Argoll Yardley Henry Mathews Thomas Roche	5
John Cole Arthur Wittington	2	Catalina (Negro)	
John Cole Sam¹¹ Church Jun.	2	Wm Lawrence Tho: Belsford	2
John ?	1	Col. John Stringer Robt. Chew Tho: Oxford	8
Wm Bennett	1	Tho: Worcham Rich: a Boy	
John Mapp ? ?(Negro) ? ?(Negro)	3	John Johnson Canutus Bence	2
Thomas Kendall John ?	2	Rich: Hanby	1
Wm Hickman Joseph Hickman Thomas ?	3	John Daniell Alex: Duem Jack (Negro)	3
Dunkin Micknabb	1	Tho: Sheppard Tho: Sheppard Jun.	2
John Plumb Michaell Graves	2	John Wilkin	1
Phillipp Mongon Mary Mongon	2	Will: Savage Arthur Bowzer	2
John Clarke	1	Tho: Harminson Daniell Call Geo: Jenkins Wm Sharpe Nan (Negro)	5
Richard ? Anthony Blaze	2		
John Tatum Cornelius Berry	2	John Francisco Christian his wife Grace Susana	3
Wm Hudson	1	Francis Pane (Negro)	1
John Floyd Abraham Sheppard	2	Daniell Payne	1

Samuell Church	1	Francis Pettitt Justinian Pettit John Hornesby	3

Mr. John Robins
  Rich: Robins
  4 Negroes
	6	Charles Parkes
		Joseph Parkes
			2

Mrs. Robins Family
  John Symonds
  John Wooten
  2 Negroes
	4	Lieft. Coll. Wm Water
		  Edward Joanes
		  Ed: Evens (att Hopkins)
		  Sam: Hande
			12

John Webb
  Samuell England
  Tho: Arundell
	3	James Stamps
		Wm Pagett
		Jacob Chilton
		Geo: Treherne	

Nath: Wilkins
  Rich: Cox
  Geo: (Negro)
	3	Tho: Viner
		John Cowan
		Wm (Negro)
		Besse (Negro)
			3

Mrs. Vosses
  Tho: Coffin
  Nan (Negro woman)
	2	Will: Starling
		Will: (a servant)
			2

Arian Francisson	1	Will: Paule	1

Lieft. Coll. Wm Kendall
  Geo: Mortimer
  John Tankerd
  James Harrison
  Wm Lewis
  Cornelius Areele
  Peter Morgan
  Morgan Thomas
  Walter Mannington
  John Harris
  Rich: Richards
  Thomas Realy
  Mathew Williams (Seaman)
  Seaven Negroes
	20	Province Nelson
		
		Wm Smith
		  Tho: Hemmins
		
		Robt. Blake
		
		Nicho: Powell
		  Wm Line
		  Damon Nahaculin
		  Rich: Williams
		
		Mr. John Michaell
		  Edw: Corkitt
		  Robt. Warborton
		  John Aleworth
		  Wm Gray
		  Anthony
		  Seaven Negroes
			1
			
			2
			
			1
			
			4
			
			13

Jerom Griffith	1		
Walter Mathews	1		
Andrew Smaw	1	John Knight Jonas Dixon	2

John Dormon
  John Margett
  Lewis Williams
	3	Geo: Freshwater
		  Rich: Quinch
			3

John Mills	1	? (a Negro)	

Wm Mellinge	6		Wm Harper	4
Robt. Filkin			Hen: Morgan	
Peter Vickar			Rowland Williams	
Jacob Glasfeild			Jonas Wetherly	
Isaac Vinam				
John Wyer			Thomas Moore	4
			John Moore	
Maior Wm Andrews	4		Tho: Somersett	
Tho: Farnell			James Beckett	
John Price				
Wm Kinge			Tho: Poynter	2
			John Hawkins	
Wm Geldinge	3			
Luke Geldinge			John Adolfph	3
Charles Geldinge			John Fotheringe	
			Benony Ward	
Joseph Warren	1			
			Alex: Mills	1
John Waterson	4			
John Wilshire			Eustis Sanders	2
James Bowzer			Daniell Neech	
John Moore				
			Francis Harper	2
Wm Harman (Negro)	2		Walter Carter	
Jane (his wife)				
			Thomas Hogg	3
Manuell Drigges (Negro)	1		Tho: Coleman	
			Abrahanm Collins	
Bartholomew Cosier	1			
			John Stevens	1
Thomas Blacklock	1			
			Thomas Harmar	1
Dennis Omelegon				
			Thomas Clay	1
Will: Senior	1			
			Basshaw Ferdinando	3
Tho: Parnell	1		Susan (Negro)	
			Hanna (Negro)	
Mr. Francis Piggott	6			
Dormon Loughland			Hen: Marshman	2
Howell James			John Watts	
Tho: Carter				
Jone George			Tho: Scot	1
Old Jack				
			Edw: Ennis	2
Tho: Bells	1		Hen: Michell	
Bastian Cane (Negro)	2		Wm Ennis	1
& his wife (Negro)				
			Neale Mackmulin	2
King Tony (Negro)			John Jewitt	

Jeremy Robinson	4		Dermon Fox	3
Wm Bellamore			Denham Olandum	
Robt. Smith			Edm: Allen	
Judith (Negro)				
			George Smith	1
Tho: Swindall	1			
			John Mattin	3
Robt. Hayes	1		George Lillee	
			John Wappell	
Mathew Pippin	1			
			John Allen	1
Teage Odeere	2			
John Marian			Capt. Custis famely	
			Will: Baker	14
John Bagwell	1		John Robinson	
			Tho: Skinner	
Tho: Hunt	4		Nich: Salmon	
John Shallicome			Hen: Foreman	
Wm Shore			Milnl Stone	
John Daniell			Tho: Jones	
			Charles Wrissel	
Geo: Isdell	1		Daniell Swindoll	
			Daniell (Negro)	
Francis Williams	3		Gabriell (Negro)	
Hen: Williams			Besse (Negro)	
Rich: Tatlock			Babb (Negro)	
			Charles Holden	
Harman Johnson	1			
Rich: Whitmarsh	4			
Wm Cord				
Robt. Holliday				
Sam: Ammett				

"A List of Tythables in North^ton County Anno Dom 1668 delivered in att a Court held in the sd County the 28th of August 1668." (Northampton County OB p54, f54, p.55, 1668.)

Samson Robins
  Luke Fountam
	2	Mr. Will: Whittington
		  Tho: Foscue
		  Rich: Beard
			9

John Dolby Sen.
  John Dolby Jun.
  John Read
	3	Cornelius Harman
		  Will: Abbott
		  Will: Sardon
		  John Collings	

James Sanders
  John Dalby
  John Robins
	3	Twoo Negros
		
		Walter Mills
			
			1

Arthur Upshott
  Isaack Jacob
  Richard Coston
  Will: Adwane
  Rich Jeffry
  Will: Becker
  Rich: Antonum
	7	John Haggaman
		
		Will: Gaskin
		  Robt. Gaskin
		  Robt. Butler
		  Nath: Stakey
		  Geo: Bynam
		  A Negro woman
			
			7

Armstrong Foster Tho: Evans	2	Robt. Elias John Senhouse	 1

James Davis Sen.
  James Davis Jun.
  Wm Grevavill
  Abraham Bonage
  Stephen Lang
  George South
	6	Tho: Bullock
		  Tho: Lukas
		
		Robt. Widgin
		  Rich: Wildgoose
			2
			
			2

Thomas Davis
  Perce Davis
	2	Teage Harman
		  John Glasswell
		  Rich: Watkins
			3

Francis Darby	1	Tho: Norly	1
Patrick Strelly	1	Tho: Bagley	1

John Kendall
  John Abraham
  John Weriers
  John Thomell
  Hen: Newton
	5	John Furrs
		  Ralfp Warnell
		
		Rich: Nottingham
		  Will: Ewin
		  Tho: Owen
			2
			
			3

Arthur Armtrading
  Rich: Garrison
  Owen Howell
  Francis Roberts
	4	Mathew Houslett
		  Peter Watson
			2

Will: Foster
  John Sancis
	2	Beniamine Cowdree
		  Will: Cowdree
		  Mathew Patrick
			3

Robt. Foster	3	Will: Stevens	4
Armstrong Foster		Hen: Reade	
Martin Oaks		Morgan Poldinge	
Tho: Estmed	1	John Dawson	
John Stockely	2	Peter Lang	2
Will: Stockely		Jacob Hill	
John Wimbrough Jun.	1	Will: Westerhouse	3
		Adrin Westerhouse	
Tho: Dunton	1	Lawrence ?ior	
Will: Satchell	2	Robt. Twilly	1
John Satchell			
		Amos Garris	1
John Evens	2		
Rich: Gilbert		John Whitehead	2
		Robt. Miller	
Leift. Isaack Foxcroft	6		
John Hudson		John Walter	2
Jack (an Indian)		Jeremy Walter	
Tony (Negro)			
Humphry (Negro)		Edm: Joyne	2
Sissaly (Negro woman)		Robt. Walter	
Simon Foscue Sen.	3	Hen: Hall	1
Simon Foscue Jun.			
Isaack Russell		Rich: Robins	2
		Tho: Farnell	
Capt. Will: Jones	3		
John Lukas		John Wimberough Jun.	2
Harman Johnson		& a Servant	
Nicholas Granger	2	Geo: Borer	1
John Croply			
		Phillipp Mangum	2
John Mapp	3	Mary Mangum his wife	
Tho: Collins			
Will: Tipshott		Rich: Aust	1
John Lyon	1	Tho: Dimmer	2
		Will: Amond	
John Wilson	1		
att Edw: Stevens Const.		Will: Lawrence	2
		Tho: Belsford	
Abraham Vansoult	2		
Will: Cox		John Clarke	1
Hen: Mathews	1	Cornelius Berry	1
Will: Hickman	3	John Johnson	1
Joseph Hickman			
Tho: Rice		att John Stringer	3
		Tho: Wilson	
Walter Price	1	Rich: Curtyse	

John Parsons	1		Mr. Tho: Ridinge	8
			Mr. Argoll Yardly	
Rich: Patrick	3		Tho: Kendall	
John Dickason			John Hudson	
John Dendy			Tho: Roach	
			Catalina (Negro)	
Joseph Godwin	2		Mr. John Mansfield	
Casar Godwin			Mr. John Harrison	
Will: Kennett	1		John Wilshire	1
Edw: Kalle	1		Tho: Harmison	6
			Edw: Ashby	
John Abbott	2		Geo: Jenkins	
Tho: Church			Dan: Crord	
			Will: Sharpe	
Samuell Church	1		Nan (Negro woman)	
John Basy	2		Tho: Sheppard Sen.	2
John Blanck			Tho: Sheppard Jun.	
Will: Hudson	2		John Daniel	5
Tho: Jarvis			Alex: Dum	
			John (Negro man)	
Jacob Bishopp	1		Mingo (Negro woman)	
			Frank (Negro woman!)	
Robt. Harrison	1			
			Charles Parkes	2
John Floyd	2		Joseph Parkes	
Abraham Sheppard				
			Daniel Pane	1
John Tatum	2			
John Hornsby			John Mills	1
Rich: Dibbins	1		att Mrs. Vosses	2
			Tho: Coffin	
Geo: West	1		Nan (Negro woman)	
John Plomb	2		att Lidia Wilkins	1
John Merriweather			Tho: Cooper	
Francis Pettitt	1		John Margett	1
Dunkin Macknabb	1		Rich: Hanby	
Christopher Stanly	1		Nath: Wilkins	3
			Rich: Cox	
Christropher Turner	1		Geo: (Negro man)	
Robt. Hopkin	1		John Webb	2
			Tho: Arundell	
John Cole	2			
Rich: Richards			John Parnnell	1
Rich: Foster	2		Francis Pane (Negro)	1
Sam: Powell				

John Duparkes	1	John Francisco (Negro)	
		Christian his wife	
Peter Duparkes	2		
Rich: Duparkes		Will: Lyne	2
		Wid. Judget	
Capt. John Savage	4		
Tho: Ranks		Peter Nathews	1
John Ames			
Tempus Betha		Andrew Smaw	
Mr. John Robins	6	att Mrs. Robins	2
Mathew Dorman		Tony (Negro)	
Jack (Negro man)		Jack ?	
Bess (Negro woman)			
Congo (Negro man)		Syan Geere	
Songo his wife			
		Wm Paule	1
Will: Morris	1		
		Dennis Omelegon	1
Leift. Coll. Wm Kendall	8		
John Tankerd		Leift. Coll. Wm Walters	10
Cornelius Arreale		Geo: Treherne	
Peter Morgan		Tho: Viner	
Jasmes (Negro)		John Cowan	
Charles (Negro)		John Fisher	
Nan (Negro)		Edw: Evens	
Frank (Negro)		Stephen Avis	
		Sam: Handee	
Nicholas Powell	3	Will: (a Negro man)	
Rich: Williams		Besse (a Negro woman)	
Robert Hollyday			
		Will: Harper	3
Mr. Provice Nelson	1	John Fathery	
		Walter Jones	
att Bartho: Cosier (Constable)	1		
Derman Howelinge		Henry Marshman	3
		James Weatherly	
John Waterson	4	John Lyellinge	
Edw: Crockett			
John Moore		Robt. Hayes	2
Lewis Jackson		John Dorman	
Joseph Warren	1	Mathew Pipping	1
Robt. Blake	1	Teage Odeer	1
Will: Smith	2	Edward Ennis	2
Tho: Hennings*		John Jewett	
Will: Harman (Negro)		Will: Ennis	1
& his wife			
		Hen: Mitchell	1
Manuel Rodriggus (Negro)	1		

Will: Starling	3	Jeremy Robinson	4
Wm Charleton		Tho: Jones	
John Curtis		Robt. Smith	
		Judith (a Negro)	
Will: Geldinge	3	Geo: Smith	2
Charles Geldinge		Geo: Lilly	
Luke Geldinge			
		Tho: Clay	1
Rich: Whitemarsh	3		
Sam: Samuell		Tho: Harman	2
Rich: Curtis		Evan Jones	
Mr. Wm Andrewes	3	Beniamine Ward	1
John Peirce			
Wm Kimge		Denham Olandum	3
		Dormon Foy	
Wm Mellinge	7	John Marian	
Tho: Heder			
Jacob Glanfield		John Morre	1
Owen Marsh			
Peter Vickar		John Bagwell	2
Frank Amam		Will: Daniell	
John Wyer			
		Bastian Cane (Negro)	2
Mr, John Willett	1	Grace his wife (Negro)	
James Stampe	2	King Tony (Negro)	2
Thomas Stampe		Sara his wife (Negro)	
Tho: Blacklock	1	John Allen	1
Mr. John Michael	11	Geo: Freshwater	3
Rowland Williams		John Coleman	
Wm Collins		Old Dye (Negro)	
Nath: Jones			
Wm (Negro man)		Bashaw Ferdinando (Negro)	2
Wm (Negro man)		Susan his wife (Negro)	
? ?			
? (Negro woman)		John Adolph	2
Besse (Negro woman)		Jonas Dixon	
Jane (Negro woman)			
Tango (Negro)		John Knight	1
Alex: Mills	1	Tho: Morre	5
		John Somersett	
Neale Mackmullin	1	James Bookett	
		John Smothers	
Att Mathew Gittiongs (Constable)		Misni Stone	
Walter Carter	1		
		Tho: Skinner	1
Francis Harper	1		
		Tho: Hogg	2
Dan: Neech	2	Abraham Collin	
Anth: Bowzer			

Tho: Heath
  John Shallicome
  John Daniel
  Will: Shore
	4	Thomas Poynter
		  John Hawkins
			2

Richard Jacklock	1	Mr. Francis Pigott
		  Mr. John ?
		  Howell James
		  Peter George (Negro)
		  John George (Negro)
		  Tho: Carter (Negro(
		  Old Jack (Negro)
		  Justinian Pettitt
			8

Dorman Laughland			

Tho: Rodriggus (Negro)
  Sara (Negro)
  Morgan Thomas
  Walter Mannington
	4		

		Charles Holden	1

		Capt. John Custis
		  Charles Wrissell
		  Dan: Swindall
		  Daniell (Negro)
		  Gabriell Jacob
		  Barbery (Negro)
		  Besse (Negro)
			7

"A List of Tithables in the lower part of Northampton County delivered at a Court held the 28 of August 1671." (Northampton County OB f. 114 - f. 115, 1671).

Capt. Jn° Custis his List		Lt. Coll. Wm Waters his List	
Teage ODear	2	Agnes Powell for Jacob Will	1
Robt. Smith			
Stephen Cown Sen. Stephen Cown Jun.	2	Mrs. Milling for Owin Marsh John Mokye Donnie (a Negro boy)	4
Thomas Clay	1	Silvia (a Negro woman)	
Benomy Ward	1	Jacob Vanam	1
Somerset Davis	1	John Waterson William Abbott	6
Mathew Pippin	1	Jacob Glanfield John Moore	
Walter Carter	1	Tony (a Negro) George	
Onial Macmillin John Daniell	2	Robert Warren Joseph Warren	2
Thomas Moore John Smothers John Camill Anne Harman Gilbert Moore	5	Wm Gelding Charles Gelding Charles Russell	3
		Hirman Johnson	1
Thomas Sommmerset	1	Bartholemew Cosher Dermont Hiawlin	2
John Moore Wm Lewis	2	Wm Harman & ? (Negro)	2
John Morgan Rowland Williams	2	Robert Miller	1
John Knight Micaell Dixon	2	Maj^r Wm Andrews George Enilin Wm Hawley	3
Allexander Mills	1		
John Heyns Dorman Foy Allexander Chambers Tho: Driggus Sarah his wife Peter Beckitt	6	Elishiba Kenirdey for Kinge Lord Richd Warren	2
		John Mattison	1
John Tankard	1	Wm Starling John Custis Richd Basy	3
George Esdall	1		

Tho: Hunt	
John Shallgreene	
Wm Shore	
Piet^r Eliot	
Jack (Negro)	
John Houkins	
Thomas Poynter	3
James Berkitt	
Tho: Coleman	
Wm Harper	2
Thomas Skinner	
Wm Ennis Sen.	
Wm Ennis Jun.	
Henry Michill	1
Henry Markman	2
P? Morgan	
Danill Neech	1
John Willett	6
John ?	
Evan Denis	
Thomas Coales	
Jn° Cudden	
Edward Allen	
Henrick Lamberts	1
John Watts	1
Jn° T?ersey	1
King Tony	2
& his wife	
Bastian Cain's wife	
Bastrian Ferando	3
his wife	
Hannah Carter	
Miles Coulton	1
Thomas Betts	1
John Adolph	1

-40-

Richd Whitemarsh	2
Richd Custis	
Robert Nelson	2
Robt. Thompson	
Mr. John Marshalkl	12
Alex. Keelin	
Edward Abbott	
Roger Webb	
Anthony Forets	
Patrick Akins (shoemaker)	
William (Negro man)	
Tony (Negro man)	
Franke (Negro man)	
Dennis (Negro woman!)	
Nanny (Negro woman)	
Frank (Negro woman!)	
Lt. Coll. Wm Waters	12
Thomas Heddge	
Stephen Warrington	
Jn° Taylor	
Jn° Cowin	
Edwd Ennis att Hopkins	
Sam^{ll} Handy	
Stephen Avis	
Thomas Filkins	
Toby (a Negro boy)	
Bess (Negro)	
Nan (Negro)	
Mr. John Robins his List	
Nathan^{ll} Wilkins	4
Mary (Negro)	
Shabba (Negro)	
Thomas Robins	
John Danill	5
Jack (Negro)	
Dirk (Negro)	
Frank (Negro)	
Allexander Dunn	
Andrew Small	1
Walter Mathews	1
Wm. Padgett	1
Richd Hambys	2
Wm Hambys	

Francis Harper	2		Thomas Scott	1
George Byly				
			Jn° Wilkins	2
Francis Pigott	5		Thomas Cofeth	
Peter George				
Jn° George*			John Webb	5
Thomas Carter			Thomas Arundell	
James Carter			William Sharpe	
			John Ayliworth	
John Cliare	4		William Woodland	
Samuill Bennett			John Pennell	
Robert Hamilton				
Judith (Negro)			Thomas Harmon	6
			George Barker	
Thomas Grice	1		Robt. Ginnbatson	
			John Wyer	
Dermont Loghland			John Steven	
			Anne (Negro)	
Dennis Omolligin				
			Mrs. Grace Robins for	2
Capt Jn° Custis	10		John Archer (Negro)	
John Fadens			Congo (Negro)	
Danll Windall				
Wm Nichols			Charles Parkes	2
Richd Allindgo			Morgan Thomas	
Dan (Negro)				
Gabriell (Negro)			John Margetts	1
Babb (Negro)				
Gusman ?udgan			John E?ines	2
			John Billiott	
Coll. Will: Kendall his List				
			Tho: Sheppard Sen.	2
Samll Young			Tho: Sheppard Jun.	
Wm Hudson	2		William ?	2
Thomas Farbis			Thomas ?	
John Kendall	2		Richd Cox	1
Henry Lurton				
William (Negro)			John Floyd	1
John Cropliy	6		? Pettitt	1
John Lyon				
William Colly			Edward Ashby	1
Thomas Aimann				
Thomas Dillahay			Mr. Nathll Walker	
Joseph Aickman				
			Jeremy Griffith	
John Barry	3			
Wm Shore			Benjamine ?olitt	
Edward Parkinson				

Robert Hopkins Thomas ?			Mr. John Robins Tony (Negro) Cosengo (Negro) Bess (Negro)	4
Richd Dibbins	1			
			Capt. Wm Spencer his List	
Samll Church John Hornsby	2		Thomas Algood	1
Thomas Church Jun.	1		Thomas Norly	1
George West Richard Ash	2		Tho: Bullock	1
			Gorge Boarer	1
Robt. Harrison John Ames	2		Arthur Armitrading Morgan Powlding	2
Thomas Ash	1		Teage Harman	3
John Parsons	1		John Glaswell Richd Watkins	
Jacob Bishop Wm Bahkill John Baker	3		James Daby Sen. James Daby Jun. Walter Read	7
Edward Cable	1		Andrew Furlong Abraham Benomy	
Joseph Goodwyn Caesar Goodwyn Tho: S?ably	3		Edward Thomas Bryan Dought	
			Thomas Dunton	1
Thomas Dimmer Robt. Chew John Hudson Willliam Anduss	4		Armstrong Foster Peter Fountaine Thomas Foscutt Symon Foscutt	4
Richard Patrick John Robins	2		John ? John Garris Ralph Wornall	5
John Dickison	1		John Robins John Coales	
Richard Duparkes Peter Duparkes John Duparkes	3		Sampson Robins	1
Nicholas Granger	1		James Sanders George Such	3
Peter Watson Rich: Wildgoose	2		Sydney Field	
Edwd ? George Banum Andrew Aherne John Dimswan	4		Thomas Eastmiath Richd Foster Thomas Powell	3
			John Walter	1

Thomas Collins	1		William Foster	1
John Map	2		John Symons	1
Wm Upshot				
Henry Mathews	1		Justinian Pettitt	1
John Clarke			Benjamine Cowdry	6
Mr.John Savage	4		Josias Cowdry	
Cornelius Berry			Richd Cork	
Nichols ?			Moses Okrey	
? Bether			Robt. Twith	
			Geo: Latchum	
Cornelius Bowe	1		Martin Otters	2
			Robt. Foster	
Nicholas Salmon	1		Richd Nottingham Sen.	4
Tho: Castle	3		Richd Nottingham Jun.	
Thomas Lee			Wm Huin	
Jenny (Negro woman)			Humphry Read	
Wm Sarhill	2		John Haggaman	2
John Sarhill			Marnis Haggaman	
John Evans	2		Arthur Upshot	8
Robt. Gilbert			Richd Welch	
			Allex: Mattlock	
Tho: Wilson	1		Wm Baker	
			Richd Rantan	
Samuell Powell	1		James Harrison	
			Jno Harnot	
John Coale	2		Ann (Negro)	
Richard Richards				
			Richd Garrison	2
Christropher Stanley	2		Pierce Davis	
Thomas Scott				
			Wm Westerhouse	2
Peter Vicars	1		Lawrence Schyn	
Phillip Mongoon	2		Rob Twilly	2
Mary Mongon			Aaron Westerhouse	
Richard Williams	1		Thomas Farnell	1
Thomas Duparkes	1		John Lucas	2
			& a Negro	
John Johnson	1		Thomas Bagley	1

Argol Yardley	8
Henry Yardley	
Tho: ?	
Cornelius Harman	
Peter Boatswagon	
Bandy (Negro woman)	
Catalina (Negro woman)	
Jonathan Remond	
John Abbott	1
Abraham Heath	1
John Francisco	2
Christian his wife	
Wm Morris	1
John Mulls	1
Joseph Benthall	2
Sisroe (Negro man)	
Capt. John Stringer	6
.	
.	
.(no names)	
.	
.	
.	
Capt. William Kendall	10
George Mortimir	
Richard Elke	
Robert Hodge	
John Glass	
John Ferrar	
Walter Manington	
William Jouls	
Cornelius Arriall	
John Boatman	
James (Negro)	10
Cubbard (negro)	
Thomas (Negro)	
Charles (Negro)	
little Thomas (Negro)	
Dick (Negrro)	
Bess (Negro)	
Frank (Negro(	
Nan (Negro)	
Kate (Negro)	

Jacob Jacob	3
.	
.(names missing)	
Nettert Johns	1
Tho: Davis	2
Cornelius Andews	
Capt. Wm Turner	15
Brown Herbert	
Richd Nash	
Richd Beer	
Robt. Welch	
Sam^{ll} ?	
Tho:	
Irish	
Ann (Negro)	
Frank Brooks	
Henry Greenwell	
Jno Collins	
Adwolf (Negro)	
John Abraham	
Patrick ? (a Dutch boy)	
Capt. Frank Foxcroft's List	
Griffeth Sabago	2
Wm Williams	
Mrs. Anne Dolby for	3
Peter Dolby	
Joshua Light	
John ?	
Henry Hanbey	1
Edmond Joyne	1
Capt. Frank Foxcroft	8
Dan^{ll} Foxcroft	
Tho: L?ras	
Thomas ?	
Caesar Which?	
3 Negroes	

"A List of Tithables in Northampton County Adom 1674." (Northampton County OB pp. 273-274, 1674).

Major Wm Spencers devision		Coll. John Stringers Devision	
Arthur Upshott Wm Jacob Richd Welch Wm Cooke Richd Aubrum Richd Carvey	6	John Partout Jenny (Negro)	2
		Steven Scott	1
Nath¹¹ Nash Tho: Lyon John May Anne (Negro) Dan¹¹ Till John Smith Wm Spencer	7	Rich: Granger Junʳ John Walker	2
		Richᵈ Patrick Humphry Read Richᵈ Patrick	3
		Capt. John Savage Tempus Betha Wm Tilfare	3
Justinian Pettitt Richd Elke John Beliote	3	Wm Hudson Robt. Jarbace	2
Vrinton Foster Junʳ	1	Robt. Harman Jnº Gaubugan	2
Patrick Ardly	1	Francis Pettit Bridget (Negro)	2
Richard Jester	1		
Tymon Foscue Watt Mills John Collins	3	Jnº Stringer Jnº James ? Shepheard Wm ?.eague ? Parkinson ? (minister) Jnº Mills Dan¹¹ An?crugh James Withers Rowland Towers Vincent Roberts 3 Negroes	14
John Winberry Thomas Foscue	2		
John Winberry Junʳ	1		
Thomas Dunton	1		
Richᵈ Nottingham Wm Ewin Benja: Nottingham	3	Wm Tipshod	1
Richᵈ Nottingham Junʳ Richᵈ Watkins		Jacob Bishop Jnº Baker	2
Teague Harman John Glasswell Nath: Wilson	3	Thomas Collins	1
		Thomas Hemmings	1
Joseph Benthall Richd Core	2	Jnº Tatum	
		Jnº Hazey	1

Wm Whitington
  Symon Foscue Junr
  James Cranstone
  Tho: Williams
	4	Jn° Crowley
		  Joseph Hickman
		  Robt. Butler
		  Tho: Watchin
		  Richd (Negro)
			5

John Dolby (Irishman)	1		

Thomas Jacob
  Wm Bedder
	2	Tho: Church Junr
		  James Pettijohn
		  Gabriell Powell
			3

Fran: Brookes	1		
Henry Scott Thomas Smith	2	Sam^ll Church	1
		Jn° Hudson	1
Peirce Davis	1	Wm Baker	1

Wm Roberts
  Henry Knight
  Thomas Ast
  William Dennis
	4	John Dixson	1

		Hen: Mathews Tho: Roberts	2
Tho: Farewell	1	Edw: Cable	1

Walter Reade
  Richd Garrelson
	2	Peter Duparks
		  Richd Duparks
			2

John Lucas	1	Richd Dibbins	1
Cornewlius Anderson	1	Charles Russell	1
Francis Darlinge	1	Tho: Wilson	1

Wm Satchell
  John Satchell
  Wm Pettijohn
	3	Sam^ll Ginnge	1

		Robt. Widgen
		  Sam^ll Tracfield
		  Edw: Gunter
			3

Thomas Powell Jeremy Walker	2		
		Jn° Johnson	1
Thomas Allegood Thomas Arley	2	Cornelius Berry	1
Mr. John Abrahams	1	Jn° Duparks	

Robt. Twilley	1	Joseph Godwin
		  Tho: Laine
		  Edgar Godwin
			3

Wm Westerhouse
  Lawrence Joyne
  Aaron Westerhouse
	3		

		Jn° Abbott	1

John Luke
  Cornelius Harman
	2	Edmund Gardtes
		  Jonathan Newton
			2

Wm Williams	1		Argoll Yardley	3
			Dan^{ll} (a boy)	
John Bull	1		Harman Johnson	
Mathew Patrick	2		Jno Kendall	
James Reluck			John Burrows	
			Henrick Bowdin	
James Davis Junr	2		Wm (a Negro)	
John Whitehead				
			Wm Cowdrey	1
James Davis Sen	4			
James Smothers			Phillip Mangen	2
Andr: Hambleton			Mary Mangen	
Edw: Thomas				
			Coll. Wm Kendalls Devision	
John Furrs	4			
Ralph Wornell			Tho: Scott	3
Rhoderick Powell			Wm Scott	
John Shuht			Robt. Janes	
Geo: Baynum	1		Tho: Harmanson	6
			Robt. Grimbleson	
Tho: Smith	1		John Mayor	
			Tho: Taylor	
Thomas Evans	1		Jno Tillery	
			Nan (Negro woman)	
Wm Gascoine	4			
Henry Gascoine			Richd Hanby	2
Robt. (Negro)			Wm Hanby	
Dorothy (Negro)				
			Benja: Aydelett	1
Robt. Gascoine	3			
Robt. Elias			Jno Wilkins	1
A negro woman				
			Jno Small	1
Isaac Foxcroft	6			
Joseph Ditto			Tho: Shepeard Senr	3
Wm Bates			Tho: Shepeard Junr	
Thomas Lucas			Wm Shepeard	
John Febers				
John Hudson			Andrew Small	1
			Wm Padgett	1

-48-

Lt. Coll Waters Devision

Wm Waters	14
Tho: Heddy	
Geo: Parker	
Geo: Clarke	
Sam^ll Handy	
Edw: Hopkins	
Tho: Wilkins	
Wm Holland	
Hend: Tyson	
Tabby (Negro)	
danuiel (Negro)	
Besse (Negro)	
Tho: Pe?ton	
Tho: Chick	
Jn° Richards Senr	11
Rodger Davis	
Anth: Jones	
Robt. Browne	
Wm (Negro man)	
Tony (Negro man)	
Mingo (Negro man)	
Franke (Negro man)	
Franke (Negro woman)	
Denny (Negro woman)	
Nanney (Negro woman)	
att Mrs. Agnes Powell	2
James Adames	
Will (a Negro man)	
Barth: Cosier	4
Robt. Thompson	
Tho: Thompson	
Jn° Marriott	
Robert Nelson	3
John Aurvin	
Wm Wilson	
Wm Guildon	
Charles Guildon	
Tho: Coffin	
John ?	
Joseph Warren	2
Robt. Warren Junr	
Richd Williams	1
Nath: Wilkins	4
Tho: Cooper	
2 Negroes	
Wm Kendall	10
Tho: Eyres	
Richd Cox	
Wm Jones	
Wm Thomas	
Walter Mannington	
Tho: Paine	
Geo: Haynes	
Andrew Evans	
Cornelius Arreale	
James (Negro man)	8
Sipco (Negro man)	
Tho: (Negro man)	
Charles (Negro man)	
Dick (Negro man)	
Will (Negro man)	
Cathbert (Negro man)	
Allexan^der (Negro man)	
Nan (Negro woman)	4
Hannah (Negro woman)	
Besse (Negro woman)	
Kate (Negro woman)	
Henry Marshman	2
Jn° Taylor	
Jn° Dan^ll	5
Alex^der Duem	
Jack (Negro)	
Dick (Negro)	
Frank (Negro)	
Charles Parks	4
Henry Arale	
Robt. Williams	
John	
Jn° Webb	3
Jn° Hahe	
Hen: More	
Walter Mathews	1
Nath: Walker	1

att Mrs. Anne Mallinges   4
  Wm Marsh
  Benja: Salt
  Tho: Fidler
  ? (a Negro)

att Mrs. Andrews   3
  Geo: Evelin
  Robt. Lowe
  Wm ??

Coll. Custis his Devision

Wm Harper   2
  Tho: Cole

Basher Fernando   3
  Susan his wife
  Hannah Carter

Tho: Hall   2
  Sam¹¹ ?

Teague Edward   1

Tho: Clay   1

John Moore   1

Rich: Tatlock   1

Jnº Clere   6
  Rihᵈ Land
  Walter Talbitt
  Tho: Goodson
  Robt. Humbleton
  John Browne

Robt. Hayes   1

Steven Costin Senʳ   2
  Steven Costin Junʳ

Tho: Hogg   3
  Robt. Smith
  Tho: Coleman

? (Negro woman)   1

Robt. Millor   1

Edw: Calcutt   1

Wm Harman (Negro)   2
  Jane his wife (Negro)

Jnº Robins   6
  Tho: Viker
  Congo (Negro man)
  George (Negro man)
  Songe (Negro woman)
  Besse (Negro woman)

Mrs. Grace Robins family   3
  Jnº Arcter (Nergo)
  Tony (Negro)
  Jnº Green

Coll. Custis' Division (Continued)

Tho: Hunt   7
  6 more

Jnº Glasse   1

Neale McMillon   3
  Jnº Daniell
  Jnº Hucker

Thomas Moore   6
  Jnº Smothers
  Gilbert Moore
  James Buckett
  Jnº Camell
  Anne Harman (Negro)

Dorman Loughland   1

att Jnº Willett   5
  Geo: Russell
  Roger Groves
  Wm Pilehard
  Tho: Haggers

Mr. Pigott 4 Negros	5	Jnº Custos Senʳ Jnº Custis Junʳ Ben: Robinson Wm Michaels Owin Hughes Jnº Brewer Robt. Newton Adam Moxon Geo: Murphy Batt Enmalls Danˡˡ Swindall Wm Ayre Danˡˡ (Negro) Gabrieˡˡ (Negro) Tom (Negro) Jeffry (Negro) Joane (Negro) Bab (Negro) Isbel (Negro) Charles Couch	20
Dennis Amulegan	1		
John Watts	1		
Richᵈ Whitemarsh Jnº Thomas	2		
Richᵈ Curtis Steven Abill	2		
Jnº Eyres 3 Negroes	4		
Jnº Marian			
Derihann Allondius Dermon Joy	2		
Wm Lowe	1	Ralph Deane Richard Aldridge	2
Tho: Sumersett	1		
Geo. Freshwater Senʳ Geo: Freshwater Junʳ	2	Danˡˡ Neech Eustis Sanders	2
Jnº Hawkins	1	Coll. Stringers List wantinge	
Jnº Knight	1	Wm Lawrence Constable-parish	1
Major Spencer wantinge in his List		Tho: Church Senioʳ	1
Michaewl Rickards	2	James Bruce - parish	1
James Sanders	2	Tho: Cowdery (fathers house)	1
Wm Sercio (forgott)	(1)	Jnº McKay (Wm Cowderys house)	1
Marcus Hagamond	1	Coll. Kendalls List	
Sam: (Ropemaker)	1	Jnº Margett	1
Hewrick Abell	1	Jnº Viker	1
Lambert Groton	1	Jnº Powell	1
att Walker by Danˡˡ Bucknam	1	Edw: Ashby (Mrs. Robins her house)	1

Mattise Williams	1		Lt. Coll. Walters	
Wm Gildrion Junr	1		Robt. Warrren Senr	1
Amos Garries	1		Henry Warren	1
Coll. Custis			Jn° Waterson	4
Walter Carter	3		Jn° Koyd	
Mathew Pippin	1		Jacob Greenfield	
			6 for ye minister	
Wm Sharpe	1		Mr. Green	4
George Frizell - parish	1		John Tyhe	1
Bust (his widow)	1		Wm Abbott	1
Kinge Tony	3		Sterlings	2
his wife				
Sarah Rodriggus			Paule Trendall	1
Manuwell Rodriggus	1		Blacklock	2
Charles Holdrin (att Custis his house)	1		Isaac Vinam	1
			Peirce Dillinger	1
Jn° Robinson (att Coll Custis his house)	1		Robt. Filkins	1
Gustman (Coll. Custis his house)			Wm. Andrews	1
Wm Oswald (Cleres house)	1			
John Isaacs (att Custis his house)	1			
Mary Rodriggus - parish	1			
Franke Costin	1			
John Curtis	1			
Jeremy Griffy	2			
Custis Persons	1			
George Lilley	1			
Benomy Ward	2			
Edm: Allen				

Sarah Driggus	1
Esdell (Constable) - parish	1
Wm Woodland	1
Hewrick Lammertson	1
Geo: Willis - parish	1
Tho: Greene - parish	1
Jnº Adolph & Michaell Dixon	2
Sandy Miles	1
Henry Pike	1
James Pada	1

"The List of Tithables in Northampton Anº 1675." (Book XII, p. 73-75).

Capt. Foxcrofts Devision		Coll. Stringers Devision	
Samson Robins	1	John Cropley	3
		Joseph Hickman	
Wm Williams	1	Tho: Warchin	
Wm Westerhouse	3	Robt. Foster	1
Lawrence ?			
Jnº Winberry		Tho: Church Junr	2
		James Petti:John	
Robt: Twilly	2		
Mathew Hollt		John Tatum	1
Aaron Westerhouse	2	Att Robt. Harrisons (Consta:)	
a hired man		John Coleman	2
		John Gawahgan	
Andrew Andrews	2		
Humphry Brooks		Thomas Bankes	1
Cornelius Harman	1	Steven Scott	1
Thomas Foscott	1	John Kendall	4
		John Robins	
Jnº Luke	1	Henry Newton	
		& a Negro	
Samll Tomlinson	3		
Marcus Hagaman		Samll Church	2
a negro		Wm Baker	
John Abraham	1	John Baley	1
Tho: Eastmead	1	Tho Church Senr	1
Tho: Farnell	3	Samll Younge	1
Rhodrick Powell			
Jack an Indian		Teigue Harman	4
		John Glasswell	
Mathew Patrick	2	Abm: Collins	
& his man		Mathew Wilson	
Henry Gaskins	5	Att Richd Nottingham Senr (Const:)	
Robert Elias		Benja: Nottingham	2
3 Negroes		Wm Ewin	
Joseph Benthall	2	Richd Nottingham Junr	2
Richd Seare		Richd Wattkins	
Jeremy Walter	1	Mich: Granger Junr	2
		John Walker	
John Whitehead	2		
Jnº his son		Hen: Mathews	2
		Walker Talbutt	

Thomas Smith	2		
Hen: Scott		Arg: Yardley	3
		Harman Johnson	
Tho: Edwards	2	Lett° Boswaine	
Cesar Godwin			
		Richd Patrick Senr	3
Major Spencer	10	Richd Patrick Junr	
Robt: Lewis		Humphry Reade	
Nich: Rash			
Jn° Collins		Edward Cable	1
Wm Foster			
Tho: Onea		Jn° Hudson	2
Tho: Taylor		Andr: Evans	
Peter Smith			
Punchanella (Negro)		George Baymon	1
Nan (Negro)			
		Tho: Collins	1
Isaac Foxcroft	4		
Wm Betts		Tho: Wilson	1
Tho: Lucas			
Tho: Fenas		Peter Duparkes	1
Wm Wittington	5	Charles Russell	1
Tho: Bushell			
Ralph Warnell		Richd Duparkes	1
Jn° Hudson			
Tho: ye Welshman		Edm: Yardley	2
		Tho: Fox	
James Dabe Senr	5		
Walter Reade		Henrick Abell	1
John Smothers			
John Foster		Robt. Widgeon	1
Andrew Hambleton			
		Wm Tipshott	1
Tom Roberts	4		
Tho: Norley		Jn° Stringer	14
Henry Knight		Jn° James	
Chrisp: Penn		Wm Streaur	
		Edw: Perkinson	
Justinian Petitt	1	John Mills	
		Vincent Roberts	
James Rollick	1	Wm French	
		Marmaduke Minller	
Peirce Davis	2	James Withey	
Robt. Butler		Joshua Crosbey	
		Mingo (Negro)	
John Seinort	12	Anne (Negro)	
		Bridgett (Negro)	
Phillipp Jacob	1	Tabitha (Negrro)	
Tho: Alegood	2	Joseph Godwin	2!
Tho: Junr			
		Wm Service	1
Tho: Jacob	2		
& his man		Tho: Hemmings	1

Michael Ricketts	3	Wm Cowdrey	2
Andrew Winter		Jn° Mackay	
Richd Bockett			
		Sam^{ll} Powell	1
Tho: Dunton	1		
		Abm: Shepheard	1
John Lucas	1		
		Rowland Towersey	1
Anos Garris	1		
		John Baker	1
Edward Scade	1		
		Tempus Betha	1
John Furrs	4		
James Nevell		John Johnson	1
Arthur Ebbott			
Mar: Simpson		Cornelius Berry	1
Arm: Foster	1	Richd Dibbins	1
John Bull	1	Fehr Viccary	1
Symon Foscott Junr		Tho; Duparkes	1
Francis Darlinge	1	Jn° Duparkes	1
Geo: Sutch	1	Gabriell Powell	1
James Baby Junr	2	Capt. John Savage	3
Jn° Garretson		Lambert Groton	
		Wm Telfaire	
Morgan Pouldrin	1		
		Francis Pettitt	2
Mrs. Dalbys Family	2	Dan^{ll} Mackrogh	
Arthur Upshoare	9	Steven Avis	1
Wm Jacob			
James Harrison		John Burroughs	1
Wm Cooke			
Richard Antrum		Tho: Owen (at Capt.Savages)	1
Arthur Gall			
Richd Carbie		Coll. Kendalls Devision	
James Carpenter			
& a negro		Jn° Daniell	5
		Alex: Dunn	
Jn° Dalby	2	Black Jack	
Tho: Aust		Black Dick	
		Frank (Negro man)	
Edward Gunter	2		
Francis Branston		Charles Parkes	2
		Robt. Williams	
Thomas Withee	1		
		John Ancell	1
Francis Brookes	1		

Mr. Benja: Cowdrey	4	Tho: Scott	3
Josias Cowdrey		Wm Scott	
Tho: Cowdrey		Robt. Jones	
Robt. Smith			
		Wm Satchell	3
John Hutchinson (glasier)	1	Jnº Satchell	
		Wm Petti:John	
Richd Jester	1		
		Hen: Marshman	2
Thomas Powell	1	John Taylor	
Lt. Coll. Waters Devision		Richd Hanby	2
		Wm Hanby	
Richard Williams	1		
		Tho: Shepheard Senr	3
Tom Guldon Senr	2	Thº Shepheard Junr	
Tom Guldon Junr		Wm Shepheard	
Joseph Warren	3	Jnº Robins (Gent.)	6
Robt. Warren		Thº Viker	
Henry Warren		Congo (Negro)	
		Colongo (Negro)	
		Tony (Negro)	
Tom Sterling Senr	4	George (Negro)	
Tom Sterling Junr			
At Jnº Bellamy		Mrs. Grace Robins famely	3
Charles Powell		John Archer	
		Besse (Negro)	
Charles Guldon	3	John Gerry	
Tho: Coffin			
John Fluellin		Henry Neake	2
		Benj: Idulett	
Robt. Browne	1		
		John Vines	1
Bartholº: Cosier	4		
Robt. Thompson		Jnº Margett	1
John Marriott			
Edw: Porter		Dan^ll Neech	2
		Eustiss Sanders	
John Mathiasson	1		
		George Lilley	1
Geo: Clarke	1		
		Nath: Wilkins	5
Mrs. Andrews famely	3	Mary (Negro)	
George Edelin	3	Shabba (Negro)	
Wm Andrews		John Wescott	
Wm Hull		John Hanson	
Tho: Blacklock	1	Mrs. Voss	1
		her Negro woman	
John Penewell	1		
		Nath: Walker	1

Mrs. Powells famely	5		
James Admes		John Alphey	1
Benja: Stratton			
Tho: Thompson		John Glass	1
Jonathan Tatell			
black Will		Saml¹ Tuckfeild	1
Mrs. Mellinges famely	5	Walter Mathews	1
Wm Mellinge			
Wm Marsh		Andrew Small	1
Isaac Venam			
Tho: Fidler		Tom Gray	1
a negro			
		Wm Harman	2
Robert Wilson	3	Jane his wife	
Wm Marvin			
Wm Wilson		John Floyde	1
4 exempted on the ministers Acct.		John Wilkins	2
John Waterson		Timothy Stere	
John Moore			
John Paulo		Edw: Ashbey	1
James Wyant			
		Mr. Jnᵒ Michaells Devision	
Arthur Spencer	2		
Jacob Glanfeild		Benomy Ward	2
		Robt. Hambleton	
Wm Waters	11		
Tho: Heddy		Richᵈ Tatlock	1
Geo: Parker			
Sam¹¹ Handy		Robt. Hayes	1
Tho: Filkins			
Tho: Chick		Richᵈ Whitmarsh	3
Tho: Pettley		Wm Abbott	
Wm Hillyard		John Thomas	
Hendrick Tyson			
Toby (Negro)		Geo: Isdell	1
Besse (Negro)			
		on Agt. Rich: Ardleys Acct	-
Peter Waples	1	Henry Pike	
		William Wilkins	

Jnº Michaell's Division (continued)

Jnº Michaell Senr	11	Tho: Hunt	6	
John Hayle		John Shallicome		
Anth: Jones		Wm Shore		
Nath: Capell		Jasper Ellett		
Wm (Negro)		James Wilson		
Tony (Negro)		Jack (a Negro)		
Mingo (Negro)				
Franck (Negro)		Jnº Custis Junr	25	
Dennis (Negro)		Cha: Holden		
Maimy (Negro)		Ben Robinson		
Franck (Negro)		John Isaac		
		Robt. Newton		
Wm Lewis	1	John Brewer		
		Adam Moxam		
		Owen Hughes		
Tho: Sumersett	1	Wm Taylor		
		Geo: Murphy		
John Hawkins	1	Caleb Trumpeter		
		Baron Sheron		
James Backett	1	Samll Fish		
		Danll Swindall		
Bashaw Ferando	3	Gussman (Indian)		
Susan his wife		Charles Crossz		
Hannah Carter		Wm Apes		
		Robt. Griffith		
Manuell Rodriggus	1	Gabriell (Negro)		
		Barbary (Negro)		
Walter Carter	2	Daniell (Negro)		
Rowland Williams		Isabell (Negro)		
		Thomas (Negro)		
Teigue Odeare	1	Joane (Negro)		
		Jeffery (Negro)		
att Tho: Hogg (constable)				
Robt. Smith	1	Dennis Amulegon	1	
Tho: Clay	1	Ralph Deane (Bricklayer)	1	

Tho: Moore	5
Gilbert Moore	
Jnº Smothers	
Jnº Camell	
Sarah Rodrigus	
John Eyres	4
Peter Beckett	
Fran: Rodriggus	
Tho: Rodriggus	
John Marian	1
John Moore	1

Edw: Harper	2
Thº Coale	
Jnº Adolph	2
Michaell Dixon	
Jnº Knight	1
Geo. Freshwater	2
and his son	
Derman Laughland	1
Negroes at Capt. Pigott	4
Peter George	
Joane George	
Tho: Carter	
James Carter	
Stephen Costin Senr	2
Fran: Costin	
Denham Alandum	3
Dorman Joy	
Walter Mannington	
Neale Macmillon	2
John Daniell	
John Webb	1
John Willett	2
Roger Groves	
John Watts	1
Geo: Willis	1
Geo: Frizell	1
Alex: Camills	1
Eustace Beascris	1

"1676 Northampton County List of Tythables Virg^a." (Book XII, p. 148-150.)

Major Wm Spencer his Devision		Coll. Jno Stringer his Devision	
Andrew Andrews	2	Geo: Corbin	1
John Morgan			
		Jno Kendall	3
John Luke	2	Henry Newton	
Marcus Hagamond		a Negro woman	
Tho: Allegood Senr	1	Wm Evins	2
		Benja: Nottingham	
Tho: Norley	3		
Christopher		Richd Nottingham Junr	1
Tho: Allegood Junr			
		Mich: Granger Junr	3
Edw: Scady	1	John Walker	
		Richard Cripps	
Tho: Willey	1		
		John Basey	2
Joseph Benthall	2	Edw: Parkinson	
Henry Himan			
		Wm Baker	1
Geo: Bowzer Junr	1		
		Sam^{ll} Younge	1
Jeremiah Walter	1		
		Joseph Godwin	1
Tho: Eastmead	1		
		Teigue Harman	3
Phillipp Jacob	1	Abm: Costins	
		a Servt	
Thomas Jacob	2		
Andrew Evans		Wm Hudson	1
Fran: Brookes	1	Jno Gawagan	2
		Jno Coleman	
Jno Dalby (Irishman)	1		
		Tho: Bankes	1
Mr. Arthur Upshott	7		
Henry Knight		Steven Scott	1
Wm Cock			
Wm Watterfeild		Richd Patrick	2
Richd Carvey		Humphry Reade	
Negro Woman			
William Jacob		Mr. Argol Yardley	3
		Harman Johnson	
Jam^{tt} Tomlinson	4	Peter Bosman	
Ralph Wornell			
Joane Hagamond		Henry Mathews	1
Negro Woman			
		John Glasswell	1
John Winberry	1		
		Geo: Leicham	1
Tom Williams	1		
		Richd Duparke	1

Thomas Dunton	1
Edward Gunter	1
Mathew Patrick Wm Howard	2
Michaell Ricketts Rich[d] Meckett Wm Foster	3
John Furrs James Nevell Nich: Nash Jn° Hiredscrol	4
Wm Gaskins (constable) Henry Gaskins 2 Negroes	3
John Hutchinson Robt. Eliat Negro Woman	3
Wm Roberts Henry Knight Wm his Serv[t]	3
Peirce Davis Abm: Bonogo	2
James Davis Sen[r] James Davis Jun[r] John Robins John Foster	4
Mr. Wm Wittington Tho: Farnell Robt. Lewis John (Indian)	4
Capt. Isaac Foxcroft 4 Serv[ts] & 2 Negroes	7
Caesar Godwin John Hudson	2
Tho: Evans	1
Francis Darlinge	1
Benja: Cowdrey 2 Serv[ts]	3
Edw: Cable	1
Peter Duparks	1
Sam[ll] Church	1
Jn° Tatum	1
Charles Weassell	1
Robt. Widgeon	1
Duncan Macado	1
Hendrick Abell	1
Robt. Grunbalson Geo: Parker	2
Capt. Jn° Savage Jn° Davis Wm Tilfaire Tho: Owen Jn° Downe	5
Jn°: Hudson Jonathan Newton	2
Jn°: Dickinson	1
Tom Tipshott	1
Jn° Crossley Tho: Warchin Joseph Hickman Tho: Fox Tho: Deleiticin	5
Mr. Jn° Bellamy 4 Servants	5
Tho: Hemmings	1
Tho: Collins	1
James Spady	1
Wm Brookes	1
Tho: Wilson	1
John Mills	1

Josias Cowdrey	1	Samⁱˡ Powell	1
Morgan Poulden	1	Tho: Church Junʳ	1
Jnº Whitehead Senʳ Jnº Whitehead Junʳ	2	Abm: Shepard	1
		Gabriell Powell	1
John Lucas	1	Tho: Duparkes	1
Martin Simpson Robt. Butler Nath: Hilst	3	Jnº Duparkes	1
		John Baker	1
Cornelius Harman	1	Francis Branston	1
Sampson Robins John Abraham George Rowe	3	Abm: Vansoldt	1
		Wm Cowdrey	1
Mr. Wm Westerhouse	1	Walter Talbutt	1
Aaron Westerhouse	1	John Johnson	1
James Rollick	1	Cornelius Berry	1
Justinian Pettitt	1	Coll. Jnº Stringer Hillary Stringer John James 7 Servᵗˢ & 3 Negroes	13
Wm Spencer 8 Servants	9	
Mrs. Anne Dalby	1	Coll. Wm Kendall his Devision	
Thomas Lucas	1	John Daniell 4 Negroes	5
Symo Foscutt Senʳ (for a Negro woman)	1	George Hinde	1
Symo Forscutt Junʳ	1	Mr. Tho: Harmanson 6 Servants	7
Wm Satchell Wm Petti:John	2	Charles Parkes John Betts Robt. Williams	3
John Satchell Richᵈ Sure	2	
Tho: Powell Richᵈ Watkins	2	Henry Masinan John Taylor Geo: Penkethman Henry Mosse	4
Lt. Coll. Wm Waters his Devision		
Mr. Jnº Michaell Nath: Capel 3 Servᵗˢ & 6 Negroes	11	John Margetts	12
		Tho: Shepeard Senʳ & 3 sons	4

Mr. Robt. Nelson	4		Richd Hanby	2
Wm Jarvis			Wm Hanby	
Wm Marvin				
Wm Gibson			George Evelin	3
			Henry Cleage	
Robt. Browne	1		Richard Lester	
Lt. Coll. Wm Waters	12			
Thomas Heddy			Tho: Scott	3
& ten serv^ts & Negroes			Wm Scott	
			John Ware	
John Fallock	5			
John Batts			John Floyd	1
Tho Wick				
Jeffry (Negro)			Dan^ll Neech	4
Besse (Negro)			Eustis Sanders	
			Owen Marsh	
Mrs. Agnes Powell her famely	3		Jn° Wilkinson	
Benja: Stratton				
Robt. Tomson			Jn° Vines	2
Will (a Negro)			Edw: Ashbey	
Robt. Tomson	3		John Heale	1
Tho: Tomson				
Jno: Marriott			John Alphey	1
Barth: Cosier	2		John Wilkins	2
Edw: Porter			Tho: Coffin	
John Burrowes	5		Nath^ll: Wilkins	6
Robt. Warren			Edm: Bibbee	
Henry Warren			John Hanson	
Robt. Jones			John Wescott	
Joseph Warren			Mary (Negro)	
			Shabby (Negro)	
Jn° Waterson	4			
Timothy Stere			Capt. Nath^ll: Walker	1
Powell ye taylor				
James Wyant			Mrs. Voss for her	1
			Negro Woman	
Richd Williams	1			
			Mr. Hancock Lee	9
John Onatts Senr	1		Eustis Perasons	
			James Fisher	
Mrs. Mellings famely	3		Six Negroes	
Wm Mellings				
Tho: Fidler			Coll. Wm Kendall	12
Cettor (a Negro woman)			Dan^ll Eyre	
			Geo: Mozminer	
Wm Geldings Senr	3		Wm Robinson	
Wm Geldings Junr			Wm Denney	
Tho: Richards			Patrick (Irishman)	
			6 Negroes	

Charles Geldings
  Wm Easware
  John Fluen

Tom Kirbinge   2
  & his son

Jn° Tankard   1

Mr. Wm Andrewe   1

Richd Tadlock   2
  Wm Halley

George Clarke   1

Paule Trondall (Constable)   0

Jacob Glanfeld   1

Coll. Jn° Custis his Devision

Jn° Knight   1

Geo: Freshwater Se^n 2
  Geo: Freshwater Junr

Tho: Coleman   1

Barthol: Heirne   1

Mr. Jno: Eyres   4
  Walter Mannington
  2 Negroes

Mr, Tho: Eyres   2
  Frank (Negro woman)

Tho: Moore Senr 5
  Jn° Smothers
  Gilbert Moore
  Tho: Moore Junr
  John Camell

Geo: Frizell   1

Drew Loughland   1

Wm Lowe   1

Dorman Joy   11

Dan^{ll} Swindall   1

Capt. Jn° Robins   7
  Mr. Jn° Hibbert
  John Fathry
  4 Negroes

Mrs. Grace Robins   3
  for John Jerry
  & 2 Negroes

Walter Mathews   1

Andrew Smaw   3
  Tho: Vines
  Robt. Lowe

Wm Harman (Negro)   2
  & Jane his wife (Negro)

Mr. Fran: Pettitt   1

Henry Neale   2
  Wm Winslowe

Col. John Cutis' Division (Continued)

Steven Costin   3
  Fran: Costin
  John Costin

Jerom Griffith   1

Mrs. Willett   2

John Watts   1

John Webb   1

Manuell Driggus   1

Mr. Clere
  2 Serv^{ts}

Benoni Ward   1

Thomas Clay   1

John Moore   1

Capt. Pigott   6
  five Negroes

Dennis Amulegon   1

John Adolph Michaell Dixon	2	Sarah Driggus (Negro)	1
Alex^r:Mills	1	Kinge Tony (Negro) and wife (Negro)	2
John Hawkins Tho: Sumerfelt	2	Grace Cane (Negro)	1
John Marian	1	Mr. David Richards his Servt man	2
Baghouse (Negro) Wife (Negro) Hannah (Negro)	3	Mr. Tho: Hunt 3 Serv^{ts} & a Negro	5
Neale Mcmillen Rowland Williams	2	Coll. Jno Custis Senr Mr. Jno Custis Junr Charles Holden Wm Michaell	18
Tho: Hogg (Constable)	0	8 Serv^{ts} & six Negroes	
Teigue Odeare	1	Richd Whitmarsh his serv^t man Wm Abbott	3
Wm Sharpe	1		
Denham Alandu	1	Geo: Isdell	1
Walter Carter	1	John Curtis	1
Tho: Greene	1	John Shallicomes	1
Henry Pike	1		
Robt. Hayes	1	John Isaac Peter De la Court 2 Negros of his Serv^{t}s in Coll. Custis his famley	4
		John Pannell John Moore	2

"An° 1677. The List of Tythables in Northampton County."

Major Wm Spencer his Devision		Coll. Jn° Stringer his Devision	
John Furrs	3	Wm Baker	1
Arthur ?botts			
Edward Servt		Geo: Corbin	1
Mr. Jno: Luke	2	Peter Duparks	1
Ralph Wornell			
		John Johnson	1
Capt. Isaac Foxcroft	8		
John Hopkins		Stephen Scott	2
Andrew Groton		John Baker	
John Popler			
Tho: Harper		Jn° Kendall	4
Anth: (Negro)		Henry Newton	
Sisli (Negro)		one neg: man	
Peter (Negro)		one neg: woman	
Martin Simmons	5	John Coleman	2
Math: Holst		Tho: Banks	
John Suthward			
Tho: Harbrow		John Tatum	1
John Servt			
		Dunkin Mcnab	1
Joseph Bruthell	2		
Richd Moses		Nich: Granger	2
		Rich^d a serv^t	
Phillipp Jacob	1		
		John Hudson	1
John Robbins	1		
		Tho: Duparks	1
Sam^ll Tomlins	3		
Isaac Hagaman		Wm Hudson	1
one woman serv^t			
		Wm Tipshod	1
John Winberry	1		
		Humph: Reade	3
Wm Williams	1	Ben: Nottingham	
		Richd Patrick ?	
Math: Patrick	3		
Robt. Edge (plasterer)		Rich: Duparks	2
Wm Howard		Gabriell Poutice	
John Hutchison	1	John Dickenson	1
Francis Brooks	2	Jn° Duparks	1
Henry Brooks			
		Edw: Cable	1
Wm Westerhouse	2		
Lawrence Schin		Tempus Betha	1
Adrian Westerhouse	2	Robt. Grimbleson	2
Nich: Nash		John Parker	

John Lucus	1		Sam:ll Younge	2
			James Gawagan	
Mr. Edmund Dalby	1			
			Coronell Arg: Yardley	3
Sampson Robins	3		Harman Johnson	
Tho: Luker			Peter Bosman	
Jno: Dueman				
			John Glaswell	1
James Navell	1			
			Wm Evens	1
James Roluck	1			
			Abm: Vansolt	1
Jnº Dalby (Irishman)	1			
			Tho: Collins	1
Tho: Farnell	2			
Jno: Witttington Jud.			Henrick Abell	1
Bridgett Sanders man	2		Jnº Davis	3
Henry Longe			James Oetti:John	
			Jnº Walker	
John Satchell	2			
his man Richd Servt			Mr. Tho: Harmanson	7
			Tho: Taylor	
Geo: Bower Junr	1		Tho: Tyler	
			Jno: Tylary	
Major Wm Spencer	8		Jnº Gray	
Mr. Jnº Abrahams			Richd Spratt	
Tho: Foscue			Sam (a Negro)	
Tho: Maye				
Peter			Teigue Harman	3
one Negro woman			Abraham Collins	
Will:			Mathew Wilson	
Walter				
			Mr. Jnº Bellamy	9
Tho: Allegood Senr	2		Robt. Lewis	
Tho: Allegood Junr			Tho: Elliott	
			Charles Runnegal	
Edmon: Scady	1		Charles Powell	
			Phillipp Sanderbry	
Tho: Estmett	1		Robt. Shepherd	
			Jonatha: Ashford	
Michaell Ricketts	3		John Batton	
Richd Beckeett				
Tho: Bosse			John Cropley	4
			Tho: Warchinge	
Tho: Dunton	1		James Fisher	
			Joseph Hickman	
Robt. Foster	5			
John Coleborne			Justinian Pettitt	1
Hen: Knight				
Wm Stuplefort			Charles Weassell	1
Hoslin Jelepam				
			Phillipp Mongom (Negro)	2
Morgan Poulden	1		& wife (Negro)	

Peirce Davis
  Wm Foster
  Abm: Bunneger
	3	Wm Winsley	1

		Cornelius Berry	1
John Whitehead	1	John Busey	1
Richd Jester	1	Edw: Perkinson	1

And: Andrews
  Aph: Barrett
  John Morgan
	3	Jn° Stringer
		  Jn° James
		  Hen: Mounteers
		  Marmaduke M?
			15

Tho: Norlow
  Christopher
	2	Vincent Roberts
		  Wm Savage
		  Wm French	

Wm Brookes
  Ed: Gunter
	2	Jn° Baker
		  Morga: Lysin
		  Wm ?hipe	

Tho: Evans	1	Rich: Norrice Mingo (Negro)	
Tho: Smith	1	Anne (Negro) Bridgett (Negro)	

James Davis Senr
  James Davis Junr
  John Foster
  Walter Reade
  Joseph (a sojourner)
	5	Lambert G?ton	

		Sam^{ll} Powell	1
		John Mills	1
Humphry Brookes	1	Abm: Shepheard	1
Tho: Powell	1	John Ancells	1
Wm Satchell Will: Petti:John	2	Mr. Wilson	1
		Sam^{ll} Church	1
John Beliote	1	Walter Talbutt	1

Mr Arthur Upshott
  Wm Jacob
  Wm Waterfeild
  Richd Carders
  Two Negroes
	6	Tho: Hemmings	1

		James Spadey	1
		Joseph Godwin	1

Mr. Benja: Cowdrey
  Tho: Cowdrey
  John Farell
  Robt. Smith
  Will (ye Welsh boy)
	5	Richd Nottingham	1

		Mr. Powells negro & Francis Branston	2

Mr. John Custis Junr
  Benja: Robinson
  David Flowman
  Tho: (Negro)
  Chance (Negro)
	5	Henry Mathews	1

		Jn° Jackson	

		Coll. Wm Kendall his Devision	
Hen: Gaskins	4	Thomas Scott	2
Robt. Lewis		Wm Scott	
Robt. (Negro)			
Dorothy (Negro)		Richd Hanby	2
		Wm Hanby	
Lt. Coll. Wm Waters his Devision			
		Charles Parkes	
John Waterson	5	Robt. Williams	
Tho: Cooper			
Powell (an Italian)		John Margetts	1
James Wenit			
Benja: Corill		John Robins Gent.	8
		Daniell (Negro)	
Wm Mellinge	4	Tho: Vyner	
John Wier		Tony (Negro)	
Owen Marsh		Congo (Negro)	
Thomas Fidler		George (Negro)	
		Colongo (Negro)	
Mr. Jno Michaell	13	Betty (Negro)	
Nathll Capell			
James Walker		Mrs. Robins	2
Anthony Jones		Jno Archer	
James Carpenter		Besse	
Wm Groton			
Wm (Negro)		Jno Daniell	6
Tho: (Negro)		Black Jack	
Jack (Negro)		Frank	
Frank (Negro)		Great Dick	
Dennis (a neg: man)		Little Dick	
Frank (a neg: man)		Cavell	
Nanny (a negro woman)			
		Tho: Shepheard Senr	4
Provost Nelson	3	Tho: Shepheard Junr	
Wm Jarvis		Wm Shepheard	
Wm Wilson		John Shepheard	
John Willett	3	John Floyd	1
Samll Bennett			
Richd Cole		John Wilkins	1
Benja: Stratton	3	Nathll Wilkins	4
Richard Lester		John Wescott	
Abraham Panter		Mary (Negro)	
		Shabby (Negro girl)	
Charles Geldinge	2		
John Flewin		Mrs Vosses	
		Negro woman	1
William Sterlinge Senr	4		
Tho: Serrlinge		Capt. Nathll Walker	1
Tho: Pettley			
Henry Tyson			

Tho: Tomson	3	Wm Harman (Negro) & Jane his wife	2
John Marriott			
Edward Porter		Walter Mathews	1
John Bettie	1	Henry Mashman	4
		Edw: Ashbey	
John Tyson	1	John Taylor	
		Henry Mosse	
Wm Sterlinge	1	John Alphey	1
Joseph Warren	1	Andrew Small	1
Wm Geldinge Senr	3	Eustace Sanders	1
Wm Geldinge Junr			
Dan^ll Lewis		Robt. Jones	1
Capt. Fra Pigot	6	John Hale	1
Tho: Sumersett			
Tho: Carter		Wm Andrews	2
James Carter		Tho: ?idney	
Edw: Carter			
Peter George		Hancock Lee	9
		Wm Houson	
Tom Marshall	1	Tom (Negro man)	
		Cubbert	
John Miller	1	Sandy	
		Dick	
Robt. Warren	3	Nan (Negro woman)	
Henry Warren		Besse	
John Warren		Hannah	
Robt. Browne	1	Wm Kendall	9
		Geo Mortimer	
Wm Waters	9	Wm Denny	
Tho: Heddy		Wm Robinson	
Robt. Lee		Peter Grice	
Wm Holland		Wm Vaughan	
Morris FitzGerald		Robt. Munck	
Tho: Chicke		Wm (Negro kman)	
John Andford		Sisco (Negro)	
Richd Mooreton			
Besse (a Negro)		John Vines	1
John Penewell	1	Mr. Jn° Michaell his Devision	
Geo: Evelin	2	Wm Sharpe	1
Henry his serv^t			
		Dorman Loughland	1
Richd Tatlock	2		
Wm Halley		Wm Lewis	1
John Moore	1	Teigue Odeare	1

George Risdell	1	Denham Alandum		1

Mr. Jnº Michaell's Division (Continued)

Manuell Driggus	1	John Webb		3
Arinell Cossinet	3	Henry Pike		
Thomas Ward		Roger Groves		
Joshua Fitchitt		Jerom Griffith		2
John Adolph	2	John Fathery		
Michaell Dickson		Mr. Thomas Hunt		7
		John Shallicome		
Dorman Joy	1	John Curtis		
		Jasper Ellett		
John Bryn	1	James Wilson		
		Jack (Negro)		
Gilbert Moore	2	Diana (Negro)		
Walter Mannnigton				
		Dan'l Swindall		1
Sarah Driggus (negro)	1			
		Dennis Amulegon		1
Tony Kinge (Negro)	2			
& his wife (Negro)		Geo: Frizell		1
Stephen Costin	3	Mr. Richardson		2
Fran: Costin		& Servant		
John Costin				
		Tho: Hogg (Constable)		1
Robt. Hayes	1	John Isaac		
Rowland Williams	1	Adam Moxom		1
		Robt. Hampleton		1
Benoni Ward	2	Servt to Mrs. Cleere		
Wm Garbin				
		John Custis Senr		19
Thomas Clay	1	Wm Orton		
		Robt. Tomson		
Mr. Tho: Eyres	3	Robt. (Ye Gardener)		
Charles (Negro)		John Howell		
Franke (Negro)		Jnº Brewer		
		Jnº Northam		
Alex: Mills	1	Caleb Osborne		
		Peter De la Court		
Jnº Knight	1	Charles Croos		
		Tho: Simson		
John Moore	2	Charles Holdren		
Joseph Frilby		Jnº Middleton		
		Nan (an Indian)		
John Hawkins	1	Gabriell Jacob (Negro)		
		Bab Jacob (Negro)		
Thomas Moore	1	Dan'l Webb (Negro)		
		Isabel Webb (Negro)		

John Smothers John Camell	2
Thomas Greene	1
Edmund Bibby Tho: Coffin John Hanson	3
Geo: Freshwater Senr Geo Freshwater Junr Wm Bradle	3
Dan^ll Neech Tho: Webb	2
John Marian	1
Richd Whitmarsh Wm Abbott John Thomas	3
Mr. Jno: Eyres Tho: Driggus (Negro) Peter Beckett (Negro) Mary Crew	4
Susan Farnandy (Negro) Hannah Carter	23
Barth: Hiron	1
John Watts	1

Ned Tucker (Negro)	
Wm Ayre (Shoemaker)	1
John Hall Senr (in Law to Eustace Persons)	1

www.ingramcontent.com/pod-product-compliance
Lightning Source LLC
LaVergne TN
LVHW020100090426
835510LV00040B/2658